Taxing the Working Poor

Taxing the Working Poor

The Political Origins and Economic Consequences of Taxing Low Wages

Achim Kemmerling

Postdoctoral Fellow, Jacobs University, Bremen, Germany

Edward Elgar

Cheltenham, UK • Northampton, MA, USA

Published by
Edward Elgar Publishing Limited
The Lypiatts
15 Lansdown Road
Cheltenham
Glos GL50 2JA
UK

Edward Elgar Publishing, Inc.
William Pratt House
9 Dewey Court
Northampton
Massachusetts 01060
USA

A catalogue record for this book
is available from the British Library

Library of Congress Control Number: 2009922747

Mixed Sources
Product group from well-managed
forests and other controlled sources
www.fsc.org Cert no. SA-COC-1565
© 1996 Forest Stewardship Council
FSC

ISBN 978 1 84720 778 4

Printed and bound in Great Britain by MPG Book Group, UK

Contents

Figures

Tables

Abbreviations

2sls	two-stage least squares
3sls	three-stage least squares
CM	competitive model
EWT	efficiency-wage theory
FOC	first-order condition
GDP	gross domestic product
MT	mismatch theory
ols	ordinary least squares
pcse	panel-corrected standard errors
ST	search theory
ttgdp	total tax revenues as per cent of GDP
t1eff	effective income tax rate
t23eff	effective payroll tax rate
t1eff	effective indirect tax rate
t1gdp	income tax revenues as per cent of GDP
t23gdp	payroll tax revenues as per cent of GDP
t5gdp	indirect tax revenues as per cent of GDP
t1rel	relative proportion of income to payroll and indirect taxes
t23rel	relative proportion of payroll to income and indirect taxes
t5rel	relative proportion of indirect to income and indirect taxes
VAT	value-added tax
WBT	wage-bargaining theory

Country abbreviations

AUL	Australia
AUT	Austria
BEL	Belgium
CAN	Canada
CZE	Czech Republic
DEN	Denmark
FIN	Finland
FRA	France
GER	Germany (before 1990 West only)
GRC	Greece
HUN	Hungary
ICE	Iceland
IRL	Ireland
ITA	Italy
JPN	Japan
KOR	Korea
LUX	Luxembourg
MEX	Mexico
NLD	Netherlands
NOR	Norway
NZL	New Zealand
POL	Poland
PRT	Portugal
SLK	Slovak Republic
SPA	Spain
SWE	Sweden
SWI	Switzerland
TUR	Turkey
UKD	United Kingdom
USA	United States of America

Preface

Defining 'taxes' is notoriously difficult. This is both a sobering and a cumbersome fact. Many people would say that tax experts are the most boring people they could think of; next to scientists perhaps, which makes scientists working on tax issues to be the least sociable people on earth! But – and this what this book hopes to achieve – such difficult to define concepts are fascinating and totally remarkable objects for social scientists. Conceptual ambiguity infuses power, politics, and even violence. I have to be violently short with my acknowledgements, since there is a great many people to thank. I am indebted to Daniele Checchi, David Carey and Reimut Zohlnhöfer for letting me use their data, Pablo Beramendi, Thilo Bodenstein, Michael Bolle, Christian Fahrholz, Robert Franzese, Steffen Ganghof, Jacob de Haan, Torben Iversen, Philip Manow, Thomas Meyer, Michael Neugart, Thomas Plümper, Francis Rosenbluth, Fritz W. Scharpf and Michael Wallerstein, for helpful comments at various stages of this book project, and my two supervisors Günther Schmid and Bernhard Kittel for their help. I am most thankful to Luicy Pedroza, who shared her intellectual insights and unlimited patience with me. All remaining errors are mine.

1. Introduction

Freedom from taxation bred laziness and lack of ingenuity, declared the Comte' de Maurepas, 18th century president of the French Navy Board in a letter to the governor of Canada. (Weaver, 1914: 746)

But not only would the right to assistance breed laziness among the working classes, so too would it 'extinguish in the upper classes the sweetest and most fruitful virtue, charity, a good which, transferred into State taxes'. Louis-René Villermé, French eighteenth chronicler of the British poor laws (Smith, 2000: 1010–11)

Do excessive welfare states cause crises in labour markets, or do crises in labour markets cause growing welfare states? This 'hen-and-egg' question haunts both academic and political debates alike. In academia apologists of the free-market would confront those who uphold the insurance and equity character of the welfare state. Ideologically extreme politicians see in the welfare state either a social 'hammock' which lures workers into idleness or a bulwark against capitalist attacks of workers' real wages. In the turmoil of these battles it is sometimes forgotten that both the welfare state and the labour market depend on each other. In this book I want to follow this idea in a specific domain of the welfare state: labour taxation. In particular, I will argue that the real question in contemporary welfare states is not whether, but how welfare is financed. How does the structure of taxation affect (low-wage) workers, and why does politics in different countries lead to different tax structures? Both questions depend on each other and are, in fact, no recent phenomena.

HOW TO TAX LABOUR – AN OLD QUESTION?

Differences in the funding of welfare states have been debated ever since the very beginning of welfare statism. Bismarck's decision to organize German social insurance as a contribution-based scheme was observed early on by Lasalle and others as a major attempt to produce social security without socialism (Tennstedt and Winter, 1993). Ironically, the contribution-based revenues of Bismarckian welfare states were not the intellectual offspring of Bismarck himself. On the contrary, Bismarck favoured a tax-financed social

security system. In particular, in the first draft of the German 'Unfallver-
sicherungsgesetz' (bill for invalidity insurance), Bismarck defended the
idea of tax-funded insurance with a vocabulary which strongly reminds us
of modern critics of high non-wage labour costs:

> Aber umsonst ist der Tod! Wenn Sie nicht in die Tasche greifen wollen und
> in die Staatskasse, dann werden Sie nichts fertig bekommen. Die ganze Sache
> der Industrie aufzubürden -, das weiss ich nicht, ob sie das ertragen kann.
> Schwerlich geht es bei allen Industrien. Bei einigen ginge es allerdings; es sind
> das diejenigen Industriezweige, bei welchen der Arbeitslohn nur ein minimaler
> Betrag der Gesamtproduktionskosten ist. [. . . Das Problem aber] steckt in
> denen, wo der Arbeitslohn bis zu 80 und 90 Prozent der Kosten beträgt, und ob
> die dabei bestehen können, weiss ich nicht. (Tennstedt and Winter, 1993: 590)[1]

Current debates on the effects of taxation on employment focus on very
similar points. In the eyes of the OECD and the EU the gist of this debate
is the following (Kok, 2003; OECD, 1995): high levels of taxation reduce
incentives to work and reduce employers' willingness to hire. In interaction
with other labour market institutions they will hurt particularly vulnerable
segments of the population. In highly developed countries these are the
low skilled, that is the low-wage sector.[2] As the tax structure shapes the tax
burden of the low skilled, this argument prompts the question of design:
Which parts and aspects of the tax system hurt (low-wage) workers more
than others? We see that the current debate about the detrimental effects
of some form of welfare state funding over others was already anticipated
more than a hundred years ago. The particularities may be different, the
fear of bad economic consequences is the same.

Interestingly, the bill designed by Bismarck never passed, but was
replaced by a contribution-based proposal finally backed by a conservative-
Christian majority in the German parliament. The reason for this outcome
had little to do with finding economically optimal ways of financing the
welfare state. Rather, political parties in the German parliament feared
that a tax-financed scheme would strengthen the role of the central state
vis-à-vis the federal states in Germany. Ultimately, the decision on how to
finance insurance was a political one (Schmidt, 1998: 24). And, although
Bismarck's master plan was to introduce an insurance system, its very specific nature – which made it so prominent a role model for other welfare
states – was largely due to federalism and the parliamentary system and
not due to Bismarck himself.

In Bismarck's case, politics overrode economics. The question is whether
we see similar effects taking place today, in a time when the claim is often
made that politics – and nation states as the prime political actors –
recede in the face of international market pressures. Proponents of such a

no-politics idea argue that most of the empirically discernible variation in the tax structure is due to inflation, growth or other socioeconomic fundamentals. Hence, diverging national trajectories are driven by automatic fiscal responses (Volkerink *et al.*, 2002). Historical institutionalists enhance this argument. They claim that the important tax policy decisions were made some 100 or more years ago. From then on, the tax system evolved as a consequence of institutional path-dependencies and created political dynamics of its own (Alber, 1982; Steinmo, 1993; Pierson, 1996).

There are scholars who disagree. Early on Titmus (1974) claimed that taxation is a fundamental part of the welfare regime which in turn is of political origin. Left versus right positioning still has explanatory power in people's attitudes on public spending versus taxation (Kitschelt, 1994; Rehm, 2005). Governments follow this logic, once we control for changes in the economic and strategic environment (Beramendi and Rueda, 2007; Kato, 2003). If there are deviations from a partisan preference, these are due to the role of veto points such as Supreme Courts or Federalism (Ganghof, 2006; Hettich and Winer, 1999). Hence, all in all the left versus right is still an important description of the underlying differences in tax-policy preferences of governments (Wagschal, 2003). So, who of the two sides is right?

THE ARGUMENT

There is one crucial difference between nineteenth-century Germany and contemporary OECD countries. Back then costs could not be completely rolled-over to labour, since wages were close to what workers needed in terms of basic nutrition and accommodation. Hence it may well be that the parliament discussed two different forms of taxation on capital rather than on labour. Note that Bismarck himself was not worried about workers, he was worried about 'the industry'. Today, however, many countries provide substantive levels of public social security and have, above all, comparatively high real wages for most workers. This implies some level of decommodification,[3] that is wages are considerably higher than the level of subsistence. The economic implication of this is that incidence of major tax forms such as income, payroll and indirect taxation is largely on labour (see Chapter 3). For this reason I focus exclusively on taxing labour, for it is, perhaps unintentionally, the modern welfare state that is a key reason why most of these taxes today fall on labour. With the long-term shift towards taxing labour came complaints that labour taxation is excessive and causes disequilibria in the labour market.

Against this historical background, the no-politics idea is clearly not wrong, but somewhat misleading. Path dependencies are at work and have led to a growing welfare state. But the underlying logic differs. The conflict of interests in the tax structure is nowadays one within labour, less between labour and capital. This does not mean that tax competition on mobile capital income, globalization or the conflict between the very rich and the poor has become meaningless. But it is not the only conflict, maybe not even the decisive one, if you focus on tax structure as opposed to tax levels. Rather, there is a conflict between low-skilled and medium-skilled workers on employment and income generation. To illuminate this potential conflict, I will not analyse the employment effects of general redistribution, that is I will not engage with the old question of an optimal level of the public sector. Rather I am interested in the implications of different mixes of taxation and its consequences for the tax structure in terms of progressivity, holding the level of taxation constant. Why do countries choose different forms of labour taxation, and why do they change their strategies across time?

The politics-still-matters idea is neither false, but has usually played the heterogeneity of workers down (for a similar point see Rueda, 2005, 2006). Interests of low-wage workers and medium-wage workers do not necessarily coincide. Both segments will at times be in conflict with each other on the optimal design of tax structure, and in particular on progressivity. The reason is that tax progressivity has only straightforward redistributive effects in a perfect market economy. Only in this case higher progressivity translates into higher redistribution between rich and poor voters, and only here the preferences for progressivity follow a clear left-versus-right pattern. In labour markets with some degree of regulation, progressivity also translates into redistribution of employment and income probabilities. Lack of progressivity will strongly harm low-skilled workers, whereas medium-skilled workers are left in an ambivalent situation. If there is competition between medium- and low-skilled workers, the former will have an ambiguous stance on progressivity.

For such a line of thought, I must presume that progressivity and tax structure will have some impact on employment, albeit this impact is weak and differs from country to country. Figure 1.1 shows evidence for this. Let us assume for the time being that the ratio of income taxes to payroll and indirect taxes is a good measure for the progressivity of a tax system. Later on I will deal with this operationalization in more detail (Chapter 2), but for now we will simply assume it. Let us further assume, as is frequently done (for example Scharpf, 2000; Kemmerling, 2003), that the low-wage sector is concentrated in categories 6 and 9 of the International Standard Industrial Classification system (ISIC) which contains service sector workers. Then Figure 1.1 tells us that there is indeed a negative

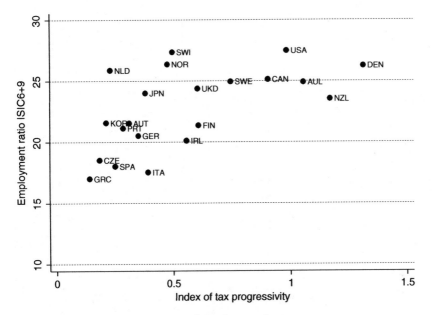

Figure 1.1   Tax progressivity and service employment

relationship: the less progressivity in the form of indirect taxation, the lower the employment in this sector.

My argument is that – to some degree – anticipated consequences and origins of progressivity are mutually dependent. Hence, the impact of progressivity on employment in regulated labour markets will also shape preferences of left parties and their major ally: trade unions. In particular, I will show that the sharper the conflict between insiders (medium skilled) versus outsiders (low skilled), and the less representative unions for low-skilled workers, the lower the degree of tax progression will be. There are two major causal mechanisms that possibly work together to explain this somewhat counter-intuitive hypothesis. First, tax progression eats up wage increases on the margin. This is particularly bad for unions when they bargain autonomously for wages with employers' associations. Tax policy is therefore similar to income and inflation policies of the 1970s and meets similar ambivalence on the part of trade unions. Second, tax progression at the lower end of the wage scale makes job competition fiercer. Progression makes take-up of work easier for low-wage earners and will put workers with slightly higher wages under pressure. Trade unions that represent the latter more than the former will therefore have an ambivalent stance also as regards activation and workfare policies.

Figure 1.2 shows a stylized empirical proof of our hypothesis. The panel

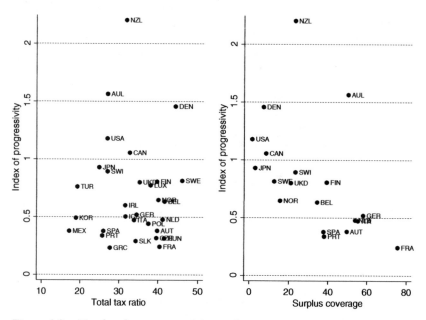

Figure 1.2   Tax burden, progressivity and representativity

on the left shows the relationship between the overall tax burden measured as total taxation as a proportion of GDP and my index of tax progressivity.[4] Again, the justification for such an operationalization will come at a later stage, here it is enough to see that the relationship between the two is not clear-cut. We see that some traditionally conservative Anglo-American welfare states have a high proportion of income taxes, and similar things apply to traditionally social-democratic welfare states. This is not new, and scholars have focused on the different characteristics of income taxes between these countries (Steinmo, 1993). I do not dispute this, but I point at the fact that political clusters are not visible in such a graph. Otherwise conservative countries should be in the lower western corner of the graph, whereas social-democratic countries in the upper eastern corner.

The right panel of Figure 1.2 shows the relationship between tax progression, as measured before, and an indicator of the surplus coverage of trade unions. For this purpose, I compiled data on bargaining coverage and union density. The indicator merely subtracts the latter from the former. The idea is that a trade union is less representative, if (a) union density is low, and (b) the outcome of their negotiation affects many non-members, hence bargaining coverage is high. Accepting this definition for the moment, we can see a negative relationship. France has the fewest representative unions and a tax system in which non-progressive tax forms dominate income taxes. The US and Denmark have a higher proportion of income taxes and similar levels of surplus coverage. The reasons differ: the US has low membership rates, but bargaining coverage is equally low. For Denmark both stay on intermediate to high levels. There are the two remarkable outliers of antipodean welfare states. I will deal with these later on, but here it suffices to say that this probably a consequence of mismeasurement rather than an outlier for my argument.

If there is indeed such an endogeneity between tax progressivity and employment theoretical and empirical approaches become difficult. My explanation needs to be parsimonious, but parsimoniousness depends on questionable theoretical and empirical assumptions. Throughout this book I will deal with these major assumptions, but to better understand them and the deductions that follow thereof, I have to clarify the underlying theoretical and empirical methodology.

METHODOLOGY AND PREVIEW

The book follows the basic mode of inquiry of political economy (for example Alt *et al.*, 1999; Hinich and Munger, 1997). I assume that policies are the result of political actors that make decisions, and the institutional rules that determine whose decisions are of importance. I will largely focus on the link between governments on the one hand and parties, interest groups and voters on the other. More decisively, I will assume certain cleavages within the electorate, especially the one between low- and higher-skilled workers. This is a common assumption in political economic approaches (Saint-Paul, 2000; Rueda, 2005). It is important to note however, that these cleavages are not necessarily entirely exogenous. To the contrary, they are part of the larger policy space in which political competition takes place and which transforms differences of voters into political conflicts (see Chapter 2).

It is also important to understand the difference between basic and final or induced policy preferences of actors (Geddes, 2003; Satz and Ferejohn, 1994). The latter are the result of an interaction between basic policy preferences and the costs or constraints of certain policies in specific situations. In particular, ever since the Communist Manifesto the basic preference of left parties is undoubtedly more redistribution and more tax progression. Yet, if tax progression entails some costs such as increasing wage competition on the lower end of the wage scale, left parties will think twice about the 'optimality' of tax progression. This form of induced preferences has to be distinguished from an underlying deeper change of basic preferences. It is certainly the case that countries differ in underlying normative and cultural aspects of taxation (Svallfors, 1997) and that these have an impact on tax compliance. However, the economic and political consequences are not at all straightforward and would unnecessarily complicate my analysis in which I focus on the costs of different tax forms.

The most important form of costs for my purposes are the labour market implications of different tax structures. Tax policies have a redis-tributive impact on labour markets, and in regulated labour markets this implies not only wages but also employment probabilities. Such effects will be anticipated by actors, albeit with a considerable degree of uncertainty. The anticipation is the ultimate reason for a potential of endogeneity in the relationship between origins and consequences of taxing the low wage sector. Again this may not seem very realistic since perception varies. Even economists do not always agree on the effects of tax policies (see Chapter 3). Nevertheless, for my purposes it suffices to say that certain tax policies have the potential to increase or decrease (low-wage) employment. After all, the expected outcome of a reform is all that political actors care about.

The empirical strategy follows a mixed methods design. Given the meth-odological problems cross-country regressions entail (Kittel and Winner, 2005), I use qualitative evidence to cross-validate my quantitative findings. In particular, I will use three forms of evidence for both origins and con-sequences of taxing low-wage sectors. First, I will use pooled regressions for some 20 OECD countries and the last 25 to 30 years. These regressions will show some of the employment consequences and some of the political origins of taxing the low-wage sector. Second, I use a historical long-term comparison – nineteenth-century Germany – to back my argument about the long-term shift from capital to labour taxation and its consequences for the induced political preferences of unions and left parties. Third, I will return to the twentieth century and compare Germany and the UK after the Second World War in more detail. The contemporary comparison of two countries allows me to test my argument on the full range of policies designed to enhance low-wage jobs. These not only include tax policies, but also labour market policies. The prime example of the latter is the use of tax-subsidies for low-wage workers.

The order of this book loosely follows the logic of backward induction. If it is true that political actors anticipate the economic consequences of tax policies, I have to start with the latter, before I speak about the former. In particular, I will begin Chapter 2 with a brief depiction of my dependent political variable. I will compare different means of measuring taxation. I will show cross-temporal and cross-country variation in the three major forms of taxation: income, payroll and indirect taxes. Finally, I will explain their relationship to progressivity as opposed to two other structural features of tax system: their insurance component, and the breadth of their tax base.

In Chapter 3 I will deal with the economic consequences of different forms of taxation. I will first survey the theoretical insights of the scholarly literature, showing that: (a) employment effects of labour taxation depend on the underlying configuration of the labour market, and (b) there is no trade-off between tax progressivity and employment in certain labour markets. I will test the latter hypothesis in a set of regressions and find that indeed some (mainly regressive) forms of taxation hurt employment more than others (mainly progressive).

In Chapter 4 I develop my argument about the political origins of tax structure and, in particular, tax progressivity in more detail. First, I will survey the literature for alternative claims about the evolution of tax progressivity. Next, I will show that key actors – voters, unions, and parties – behave no longer in a traditional left-versus-right manner, if tensions in the labour market are high. The final policy preferences for or against progressivity differs between low-wage and medium-wage employees.

In Chapter 5 I will use my three types of empirical evidence to substantiate my claims. Pooled regressions show that whereas union density has, as expected, a positive impact on progressivity, surplus coverage of union has a negative. These findings remain stable if I control for tax competition and other theoretical explanations. They also remain stable, if I control for endogeneity between unemployment and tax progressivity. The historical comparison shows that there is some truth in the claim of a shift in the underlying cleavage structure of tax policies. In the second German empire, tax progressivity unambiguously rose with the combined strength of trade unions and left parties. The cross-country comparison of Germany and the UK after the Second World War highlights a shift in the preferences of unions and left parties. In particular I will first argue that in both countries tax progressivity got under stress, once unionism surpassed its peak and became less representative for the labour force. Next I will argue that whereas the British Labour party has recently started to re-balance progressivity, the German Social Democrats are still trapped in a stop-and-go policy in that respect.

In Chapter 6 I will summarize my major findings, before I will evaluate them from a normative point of view. It is obvious that there is no clear (Pareto-efficient) political winning strategy in reforming the tax incentives to work. Neither is there a one-size-fits all approach. However, there are clearly discernable political choices, and for a reformist left Labour party high employment and tax-based redistribution are not incompatible in an era of globalization.

NOTES

1. 'For freedom is nothing but death! If you don't want to reach into your pocket and the treasury, you will not achieve anything. To impose the whole burden on industry, I don't know whether it could stand that. It would hardly work for all industries. For some it may work: for those in which the wage of workers is just a small component of the entire costs of production. [. . . The problem however] exists for those, in which wages amount to 80 or 90 per cent of all costs, and whether those could survive, I don't know.' (own translation)
2. Though clearly not equivalent I will use both terms 'low skilled' and 'low wage' interchangeably.
3. Esping-Andersen (1990: 37) defines 'decommodification' as a 'readiness to enable individuals and families to uphold a socially acceptable standard of living independent of market participation'.
4. I use 30-year averages for all country observations. Hence the figure shows long-term correlations between the three variables.

2. A comparative welfare state analysis of tax mixes

to tax – about 1300 *taxen* to assess, put a tax on; borrowed from Old French taxer, learned borrowing from Medieval Latin *taxare*, from Latin, and borrowed directly into English from Latin *taxare* evaluate, estimate, assess, handle, probably a frequent form of tangere to touch. (Barnhart, 1988: 1118)

(be-)steuern – *steuern* 'mit dem Steuer lenken', [. . .] *stiuren* 'lenken, leiten, (unter)stützen, helfen, beschenken, ausstatten, eine Abgabe entrichten, [. . .]' *stiuren* 'in eine Richtung bringen, lenken', [. . .] *stiuren/stieren* 'steuern, richten'. (Pfeifer *et al.*, 1993: 1359)[1]

The ultimate question of this book is simply why national governments differ in taxing (low-wage) labour. For an answer we first need to know what choices governments have when they decide how to tax labour. Second, we need to know what shapes political actors' preferences for different forms of taxation. In a political economy tradition, the latter will depend on the basic functions of taxation in a society, and the differences between different tax forms in performing these functions. This calls for conceptual work, and for 'taxonomy' in particular. A look into the etymological history of the word 'taxation' may hence be doubly illuminative.

Comparing the English and German etymology of the word 'tax', 'taxation', as the two quotes from above show, has two different roots. In one perspective, taxes are used to levy resources in order to pursue other policies. Hence, taxes are merely the means for achieving different goals, and should be considered as political and economic budget constraints. This is the traditional notion of 'tax' in English. Such a notion of tax policy is visible among both economists and political scientists who have collapsed the analysis of expenditure and financing of welfare states into one mode of explanation (for example Esping-Andersen, 1990; Meltzer and Richard, 1991).

The second perspective is prevalent in the origins of the German concept for taxation 'Steuer'. In this conception, taxes have a much more direct impact on preferable outcomes. Taxes are used to induce certain types of behaviour (say smoking less) or outcomes (lower inequality). Titmus (1974) was one of the first comparative researchers to acknowledge the interrelationship between taxation and social policy. I will start this

11

chapter showing how tax and social policy are intertwined, and why this has political consequences for low-wage employees (pp. 12–14). On pp. 14–18 I will narrow the set of choices to the empirically observable mix in three major tax forms. In the final section I will show how this mix reveals fundamental differences in the tax structure such as tax progressivity.

LABOUR TAXATION, SOCIAL POLICY AND POLITICAL MOBILIZATION

Labour taxation is not only a politically controversial topic, it is also substantively a very complex issue. It is a focal issue in the normative debate on efficiency versus equity and yet taxation is clearly not the only, perhaps not even decisive factor for employment and growth (see Chapter 3). More importantly, tax effects alone hardly matter for low-wage sectors, but their interaction with social and labour market policies does. Two 'polar' cases help us to see this most clearly: the taxation of social benefits on the one hand and tax and wage subsidies on the other. In both cases the interaction of tax and social policy has well-known effects on economic incentives. However, the interaction also has important consequences for political mobilization.[2]

To begin with the first of these polar cases some countries tax social benefits explicitly. Adema (1999) has shown that in this case gross social expenditure overstates actual transfers.[3] This is an example of the rising trend in OECD countries towards so-called tax-churning. For some economist tax experts this redistribution 'between pockets' of the same individual is an unnecessary nuisance. Rational and fully informed individuals should only care about net-of-tax transfers. In the 'messy' world of political economy, however, net or gross of taxation could matter, since this changes the nature of the political problem together with the political cleavages between those affected and those who are not. If voters all pay the same taxes – no matter what their employment status – they should care about the tax system in similar ways. Taxing benefits is therefore 'universalistic' in that it makes the electorate more homogeneous (Kemmerling, 2004). In countries that segregate the dependent and contributing population more clearly, the tax and transfer system drives a cleavage into the electorate. Whereas a recipient of non-taxed benefits should not exhibit a great deal of interest in the intricacies of direct taxation, welfare state dependents in Sweden or the Netherlands have every incentive to do so.

Now take the second case, tax-subsidies for targeted employees, such as in-work benefits. Examples of these policies are the well-known cases of the Earned Income Tax Credit in the US or the Working Families' Tax Credit in the UK. As a form of tax credit on low-wage earners, they are functional equivalents to higher basic allowances in the tax code of income taxation. Such policies usually do not appear in the social budget (Adema, 2001), so that they have been called the 'hidden welfare state' (Howard, 1997) or 'implicit social policy' (Kemmerling, 2004). The political mobilization of such policies is much different, since they are means-tested and framed as tax deductions rather than tax expenditures (Howard, 1997).

Both of these polar cases will lead to differences in political mobilization. It is perhaps no coincidence that countries that tax benefits are usually also those countries with both highest overall tax burdens and highest rate of approval for tax policy (Korpi and Palme, 1998; Schmidt, 2000; Boeri *et al.*, 2001) whereas in-work benefits are more important in countries with generally smaller governments and more resilience against the welfare state.[4]

The interaction of social and tax policies does not only affect political contestation, it has also empirical consequences. Adema (1999) elaborates that the inclusion of hidden and universalistic tax policies leads to a strong convergence of aggregate ratios of social spending.[5] This convergence stands in marked contrast to divergence in the level of tax and social policy programmes and instruments (Kemmerling, 2004; Castles, 2004). The way how (low-wage) labour is taxed, still differs markedly from country to country. Neither have cross-national performance indicators for labour markets converged. But if similar levels of net total taxation produce different outcomes, it is very tempting to look for structural elements of taxation and the transfer system as the potential origins of this divergence in outcomes.

Consequently, this book is not about a government's choice between more or less taxation of labour. Rather, the question is how labour is taxed. This is a question of tax structure and, primarily, a question about the tax mix of income, payroll and indirect taxes. Hence I delimit the choice to three major tax forms since these represent the major fiscal burden for the majority of wage earners (OECD, 1995). I neglect other sources of income such as property or inheritances. As a consequence, I do not deal with the intricacies of corporate income taxation, and the problem of tax competition along these lines (for example Genschel, 2002; Ganghof, 2006).

At the same time, the set of effective labour taxes is larger than the set of statutory taxes on labour. The reason for this is that the actual incidence of taxation is very often different from the formal incidence, that is the tax base (for example Homburg, 2003). Empirical estimations (OECD, 1990) of the effective incidence of taxation support economists who argue that income taxes, payroll taxes and indirect taxes fall, by and large, on labour (Nickell and Layard, 1999: 3037). Following this insight, I subsume social security contributions to payroll taxation, although the former are not taxes in a strict sense. In addition, I include all indirect taxes although they do not (only) affect wage earners. In the next section, I will briefly describe and depict the empirics of this tax mix, before I show how the mix is related to theoretically interesting fundamentals.

VARIATIONS IN THE TAX MIX

Operationalization

There are several alternative measures for cross-country comparisons of the tax mix: statutory rates, micro-, and macro-estimates of (effective) rates. All of these measures have certain advantages and disadvantages. For instance, some economists discard statutory rates, since both legal avoidance and illegal evasion drive wedges between statutory and 'effective' levels of taxation. Indeed, statutory rates are of little explanatory power when it comes to estimating effective tax burdens (McKenzie, 1999). Yet these rates are not meaningless. Experts in tax law can use statutory tax rates for international tax arbitrage (Ganghof, 2000). Statutory tax rates are also important signals in the electoral competition of parties, as statutory rates signal voters (correctly?) the different directions of parties' policy proposals (Besley and Case, 1995).[6] Statutory rates are less valid, however, if one is interested in the mix between different tax forms.

The second option is micro-based calculations. These combine statutory rates with information of all possible deductions and allowances to compute the effective tax burden for a representative individual or household. An important example is the OECD 'Taxing Wages' approach (Heady, 2004). The OECD reports effective tax burdens for different types of families and wage earners (OECD, 1995). Given the complexity of national tax systems the OECD measure is not always reliable in cross-country studies (Sørensen, 2004). More importantly, the OECD measure does not include indirect taxation (Heady, 2004: 27). Another possibility lies in the use of micro-data and to compute the averaged effective tax burden. Yet there is little comparative information on the incidence of indirect taxation. Even in the Luxembourg Income Study indirect taxes are only available for few countries and years. Hence, I can only use micro-data on rates as auxiliary information.

The third option is to recur to administrative tax data on the macro level. The standard measures here are tax-to-GDP ratios and related indicators. Problems of international comparison loom large in the generation of these measures. Tax bases and even GDP definitions may differ across countries (OECD, 1999b; Sachverständigenrat zur Begutachtung der gesamtwirtschaftlichen Entwicklung, 2003). A whole cottage industry has evolved to construct better empirical indicators than primitive tax-to-GDP ratios. The first landmark contribution in this direction was of Mendoza *et al.* (1994) who proposed a simple, easy-to-calculate measure of effective tax rates on factor incomes and consumption. This measure showed reasonable consistency with micro-based estimates (Mendoza *et al.*, 1994: 316). Yet, Carey and Rabesona (2002) and Volkerink *et al.* (2002) argue that Mendoza's methodology underestimates the effects of exemptions on some forms of sensitive income. Both contributions propose a new measure of their own correcting for this and other problems in the Mendoza methodology.[7]

All the macro-aggregate measures differ somewhat (Haan *et al.*, 2003), but Carey and Rabesona find significant deviations only in a few cases.[8] Cusack and Beramendi (2006) have tested several data sets in multivariate regressions and have also found few differences. Haan *et al.* (2003), finally, show high correlations among all macro measures of tax rates, whereas the correlation between the OECD micro indicator and the macro indicators is only reliable across countries but not along time series (Heady, 2004: 284).

For the purposes of this book, I will stick to aggregate data on tax-to-GDP ratios and Carey and Rabesona's effective tax rates (Carey and Rabesona, 2002).[9] The term 'taxation' follows the general OECD definition of taxes used in the Revenue Statistics and includes social security contributions (OECD 1998: 30). 'Income taxes' include all taxes with the OECD label '1000', that is taxes on income, profits, and capital gains. 'Payroll taxes' combine two categories: '2000' consists of compulsory social security contributions and '3000' consists of any additional taxes on payroll and the workforce. Finally, 'indirect taxes' correspond to the category '5000' of the OECD, that is taxes on goods and services like VAT, excises, and sales taxes. The three tax variables are a percentage of GDP (*t1gdp*, *t23gdp* and *t5gdp*).

The effective rates are based on those of Carey and Rabesona. The authors only report taxes on capital income, labour income and consumption, whereas I am interested in splitting the tax on labour income into a payroll and an income tax component and merging the latter with taxes on capital income. I do not dispose of all the necessary information to make these transformations. So my indicators for an effective income tax rate *t1eff* and an effective payroll tax rate *t23eff* are only roughly correct given Carey and Rabensona's methodology, but I expect the resulting deviations to be marginal. The effective consumption tax rate *t5eff* is theirs.[10] For most OECD countries, effective tax rates start in 1975 and end in 2000, whereas tax-to-GDP ratios are available for longer periods. With both tax-to-GDP ratios and Carey and Rabensona's measures of effective tax rates at hand, we are now able to compare the size of tax revenues and the respective rates across countries and time.

Temporal and Cross-Sectional Variation

Tax-to-GDP ratios have risen considerably in the last 40 years. Today, the average total tax ratio for OECD countries is around 40 per cent of GDP. Given that the three forms of taxation amount to 75 per cent of public revenue in most countries they form the backbone of welfare state finance. In contrast to total labour taxation, the tax mix has changed. In particular, payroll and indirect taxes have outpaced income taxation in most countries. Figure 2.1 shows these trends for the mean of all OECD countries. Payroll taxes, including social security contributions, nearly doubled between 1965 and 2002. Income taxation has remained fairly stable since the 1970s (left panel). In comparison, the effective income tax rate reached its high point in the 1980s (right panel of Figure 2.1) and declined thereafter. This shows the impact of a series of tax reforms in most of the OECD countries beginning with the US in 1986 (Blundell and MaCurdy, 1999). From the 1980s to the 1990s indirect tax rates have increased by more than

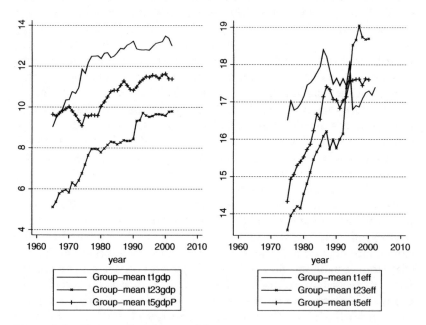

Figure 2.1   Temporal evolution of the tax mix

20 per cent. Since payroll and indirect taxes increase roughly proportional with their tax bases (see below), tax-to-GDP ratios and effective rates move closely together, whereas these ratios and effective rates differ for income taxes. This can be seen by comparing the two panels of Figure 2.1.

A look at cross-country differences in the tax mix shows no straightforward ways to cluster tax mixes. Although all four Scandinavian welfare states have high overall tax burdens, some of the continental European economies – for example Belgium and France – also exhibit high levels of taxation. If these 'average' tax rates are compared with effective microestimates of tax wedges, Italy is the welfare state with the highest overall tax burden (Heady, 2004). Clusters are neither easily detectable in the tax mix as Table 2.1 shows. It contains period averages for the ratios and effective rates of the three tax forms.

As a broad mind map, however, welfare state regimes have some merits. The archetypical Nordic welfare state is based on a universalistic and inclusive tax regime, with a high overall tax burden as well as high rates of income taxation. 'Bismarckian' continental European welfare states are based on social security contributions. Anglo-Saxon welfare states resemble Scandinavia in the sense that income taxes are usually the most important source of public revenues. These countries also use tax breaks and other hidden social policies most heavily (see above). Some authors add a fourth cluster consisting of 'peripheral-residual' welfare states such as Greece, Italy or Spain (Wagschal, 2003). This cluster is not visible in the tax mix, since Spain and Italy have tax systems that are broadly in line with those of Germany and France. For Eastern Europe it is still too early to make general judgements, but the importance of consumption taxes as a source of public revenue is clearly visible (see Table 2.1). Hence, if there is room for an additional cluster in terms of the tax mix it will be composed of Eastern European countries following the Irish model and focusing on indirect taxes.

I have performed several tests with these data.[11] Correlations for rates and ratios are remarkably high on a cross-sectional level. Table 2.1 shows that only in four cases (Belgium, Japan, Switzerland and Greece) the most important tax form depends on the use of the indicator. Correlations among the tax forms indicate that income and indirect taxes are more strongly related than either of the two with payroll taxes. This seems to suggest that income and consumption taxes are complementary political strategies whereas (so far) payroll taxes are political substitutes. Across time, one finds a high level of stability. Correlograms for the group-mean of tax-to-GDP ratios show that autocorrelation is high (around 90 per cent). For some countries autocorrelation is even close to one, a fact that prompts the question whether the tax mix is driven by strong path dependence or nonstationarity.[12] I have performed unit root tests for each country and found in at least four cases

Table 2.1   Country comparisons of tax-to-GDP and effective tax rates

Country	t1gdp	t23gdp	t5gdp	t1eff	t23eff	t5eff
Income tax as most important revenue						
AUL	*15.01*	1.47	8.11	*17.65*	3.02	12.97
BEL	*15.72*	12.96	11.74	21.69	*23.01*	17.49
CAN	*14.89*	4.23	9.83	*19.53*	8.62	15.30
DEN	*25.04*	1.56	15.54	*40.78*	3.06	26.56
FIN	*17.16*	8.00	13.47	*28.27*	16.39	22.89
JPN	*10.69*	7.53	4.28	9.00	*13.83*	6.77
LUX	*15.37*	10.70	9.19	–	–	–
NOR	*15.18*	8.86	14.96	*20.45*	18.88	25.34
NZL	*19.86*	0.23	9.34	*25.04*	1.90	15.71
SWE	*20.19*	13.46	12.01	*32.07*	23.64	19.72
SWI	*11.69*	7.07	6.00	14.40	*15.10*	9.05
UKD	*13.67*	6.43	10.80	*14.85*	11.25	15.35
USA	*12.77*	5.94	4.97	*14.37*	10.43	6.53
Payroll tax as most important revenue						
AUT	10.58	*14.93*	12.80	18.94	*22.09*	19.88
CZE	9.41	*16.86*	12.75	9.48	*34.35*	19.87
FRA	7.18	*17.19*	12.37	9.15	*31.41*	18.55
GER	11.31	*12.32*	9.69	14.31	*22.18*	14.70
ITA	10.46	*11.71*	9.87	12.90	*24.08*	14.55
NLD	12.62	*15.89*	10.92	17.02	*25.55*	17.18
SLK	7.64	*14.48*	11.74	–	–	–
SPA	6.92	*10.15*	7.45	8.07	*20.95*	11.74
Indirect taxes as most important revenues						
GRC	5.06	8.83	*11.99*	9.73	*27.46*	16.91
HUN	9.60	14.86	*15.85*	17.46	–	*24.47*
ICE	9.59	2.32	*16.85*	–	–	–
IRL	11.0	4.31	*14.03*	15.76	10.21	*20.59*
KOR	5.33	1.35	*9.58*	4.18	2.69	*15.79*
MEX	4.56	2.68	*9.45*	–	–	–
POL	11.14	12.33	*12.96*	20.32	–	18.84
PRT	6.32	7.19	*11.16*	12.43	14.39	*17.68*
TUR	6.89	2.67	*7.12*	–	–	–
Average	11.76	8.62	10.89	17.12	16.72	16.98

Note: Tax-to-GDP ratios are period means for max. 1965 to 2002.
Effective tax rates are period means for max. 1975 to 2000.
Dominant tax form in italics.

indications of unit roots. I think it is therefore justified to speak of tax mixes as a highly persistent phenomenon, that is a phenomenon which does not change dramatically across time, but which – in the majority of countries – is neither immutable. They are hence not path-dependent in a deterministic way, although paths do shape the speed of temporal adjustment tax mixes exhibit to new trends. In other words, it is politically costly and cumbersome to change the tax mix, but it is not impossible.

TAX MIX VERSUS TAX STRUCTURE

So far we have seen that income taxes are on relative decline in most countries, but also that they are still important in some countries. Is this information theoretically meaningful? At first sight it may seem that tax forms merely are nominal conventions. To answer this question, we need to know more about the economic effects of the three tax forms. On the basis of these effects one can start to reconstruct political preferences. To that matter, I ascribe three fundamental characteristics to each tax form: its tax base, its progressivity, and its insurance component. There are many more institutional differences between these three tax forms, but these are usually country-specific. I also would like to suggest the following terminology: when I speak of the set of features of a tax system – base, progressivity and insurance component – I will use the short-hand of 'tax structure', whereas I mean the triple of income, payroll and indirect taxes, when I refer to the 'tax mix'. In the following I will describe the three characteristics of the tax structure and show how each of them is related with the empirically discernible tax mix.

Starting with the first characteristic, the breadth of the Tax Base differs from tax form to tax form. The base is the specifically defined object on which taxes are levied, in our case corporate and private income, wages and consumption. Tax economists stress the idea that the broader and more inclusive a tax base is, the less it will distort economic activities (see Chapter 3). It is, however, vital to differentiate between the tax base as the sum of economic activities subject to taxation and the number of people affected by the tax. Whereas the first is more interesting for public economics, political scientists analysing voters' reactions to taxation should be also concerned about the latter.

The smallest tax base is that of payroll taxes since they only tax wages and salaries of employed people. In general this holds true, but there are important exceptions. The low-wage sector is usually more likely to be affected by payroll than by income taxation due to the former's lower thresholds, hence for low-wage earners social payroll taxes have a broader base. Also, some countries have payroll taxes that are very much akin to general income taxes. The French payroll taxes, for example, do not have caps on high incomes and the 'contribution sociale généralisée' (CSG) is levied not just on wages but on all major sources of income, and is therefore very similar to an income tax (Levy, 2000: 315).[13] The base of income tax base is larger than that of the payroll tax, since the income taxation includes not only wages but also other sources of income. It also includes more people, since self-employed and non-employed people have to pay income taxes, whereas payroll taxation is usually restricted to dependent employees. In an ideal-type world, the tax base of general consumption taxes should be even broader, as they affect all people. In the real world there are exceptions to this rule due to economic openness and exemptions in indirect taxation. On basis of a head count the situation is much clearer: general consumption taxes indeed affect all people, whereas income taxes are restricted to those with income, and payroll taxes, even more narrowly, to those with wage income.

Are these assumptions empirically correct? Estimations of the tax base on a head-count basis are very sensitive due to huge administrative differences (OECD, 2007b). One can assume – without loss of generality – that general consumption taxes have a base of 100 per cent. For social security systems it is very difficult to get comparable information, since the number of contributors differs between insurance schemes. It is safe to assume, however, that the number of those covered by public social insurance in any OECD country is smaller than the number of those in the labour force (for example Montanari, 2001). For personal income tax there is some direct information available.[14] The OECD (2007b: 124) collects data on the number of registered tax payers as percentage of total labour force. Table 2.2 shows these data for OECD countries. We see that countries differ markedly in the relative extension of their income tax base, ranging from a Korea with merely 10 per cent of the labour force paying income taxes to 250 per cent in New Zealand. At the bottom of the table there are correlations for the three tax forms with the measure of the tax base. Not surprisingly, the tax base is higher in those countries in which income taxation in general is higher. There is hence some evidence that countries with a relatively dominant income taxation have more inclusive tax bases.

Progressivity is the second major characteristic that sets income, payroll and indirect taxes apart. Progressivity is politically important for equity reasons, since it shifts the tax burden towards richer people. It may also be important for efficiency reasons, since it affects the decisions to take up work, especially for the low-wage sector. In general, progression can be achieved by two means: indirectly with exemptions such as basic allowances or deductions for those with less income, or directly with an increasing marginal tax rate. Both forms play a role for labour income, but it is predominantly indirect progression which affects the labour force participation in the low-wage sector, whereas marginal rates are more important for higher wages and for the number of working hours (see below).

Table 2.2   Indicators of tax structure

Country	Tax base	Progressivity	Insurance component
AUL	167.1	16.0	94.3
AUT	135.9	1.5	99.9
BEL	130.4	−3.9	95.6
CAN	135.4	1.5	95.0
CZE	48.6	6.5	−
DEN	158.6	20.0	93.4
FIN	184.2	9.2	99.9
FRA	124.3	−2.0	99.9
GER	69.8	6.2	99.5
GRC	223.3	19.7	98.2
HUN	107.3	9.0	−
ICE	143.8	4.8	−
IRL	104.6	19.9	94.4
ISR	−	−	−
ITA	−	6.4	99.9
JPN	69.5	11.8	96.6
KOR	9.4	11.9	−
LUX	44.3	17.3	98.7
MEX	19.5	18.3	−
NLD	84.9	−3.6	94.5
NOR	152.5	11.9	96.7
NZL	242.9	18.0	93.1
POL	163.4	0.0	−
PRT	121.8	9.7	98.7
SLK	18.9	0.0	−
SPA	186.1	−1.0	99.9
SWE	157.7	11.8	95.9
SWI	−	10.3	94.5
TUR	12.8	3.5	−
UKD	96.9	−8.9	94.9
USA	149.7	9.3	95.1
Average	116.6	17.9	96.8
Correlations			
t1eff	0.54***	0.21*	−0.45***
t23eff	−0.12	−0.46**	0.70***
t5eff	0.12	−0.03	0.1

Note: Tax base is the ratio of registered taxpayers to the labour force (OECD, 2007b), Progressivity is defined as $MTR_{167\%} - MTR_{67\%}$ (cf. text and OECD, 2004b). Insurance component is 100 minus Disney (2004)'s calculus of the pension tax.

Typically, income taxation is the only progressive tax form. For low to medium income brackets payroll taxes are proportional (Wagstaff *et al.*, 1999). People whose earnings are above a certain threshold usually do not pay contributions so that, by and large, payroll taxes lie somewhere between regressive to proportional. Again there are exceptions to this rule. Some countries have no ceiling on payroll taxes so that the formal status of these taxes is much more akin to income taxation (Goerke, 2002: 238). Moreover, some countries such as Austria and Switzerland have progressive elements in their payroll taxes (Messere, 1993). Thus the degree of progressivity for each tax forms shows some variation across countries (Wagstaff *et al.*, 1999). Finally, the progressivity of (general) consumption taxes is similar to payroll taxes. If all individuals consume their life-time earnings until their deaths, consumption taxes should be proportional to income (Homburg, 2003: 157). Many welfare states exempt certain forms of consumption such as housing rents or food from consumption taxes. The consequences of these exemptions are not clear. For instance, it is very much debated whether a VAT is slightly progressive, proportional or regressive.[15] By and large, it is hence justified to assume that general consumption taxes are proportional.[16]

There are several ways to measure the progressivity of the tax system. One way is to use the aforementioned OECD data on the taxation of high- and low-wage earners (Heady, 2004). In Table 2.2 I present such data for the year 2002–03. I have calculated the differences in per cent of the tax burden for those earning 167 per cent and 67 per cent of the average production wage. Using this indicator one can see that there is some positive correlation with the size of the income tax ratio, strongly negative with payroll taxation, and no relationship with indirect taxes. Taken together, these findings imply that payroll taxation does make it difficult to have a tax system that is progressive, whereas a high proportion of income taxes is a necessary, but not always sufficient condition of having a progressive tax mix. This is also intuitively plausible, since loopholes and exemptions in the income tax code benefit the rich rather than the poor.

Finally, the insurance component of taxes is the most intricate characteristic of the tax mix. According to the OECD (1998: 30) taxes are 'compulsory, unrequited payments to general government'. Hence, the defining attribute of taxes is their loose connection to public services. This principle is, of course, violated in the case of social security contributions, and most clearly in systems of defined benefits where contributions ensue a legally binding contingent entitlement. In this sense social security contributions are more akin to forced savings (OECD, 1995). It is for this reason that I have included this characteristic in the discussion of the tax mix. Because social security contributions are earmarked for special purposes, such as insurance against the 'risk' of becoming unemployed, sick or old, it depends on the degree of equivalence between payments and benefits whether they are taxes or insurance premiums (for example Schmid *et al.*, 1987: 93). If the equivalence is close to unity, contributions are reliably perceived as insurance and should be less distortive (OECD, 1995: 10).

It comes as no surprise that countries that have a Beveridge welfare system have far higher tax components in their tax systems than welfare states with a Bismarckian legacy. According to Disney (2004), tax components are up to 10 per cent for the UK or New Zealand, whereas they are close to zero for Germany, Austria and Italy (Disney, 2004: 293). I show these data for the latest available year (1995) in Table 2.2. Although the data are scarce one finds a strong relationship between the mix and the insurance component. Countries with high income taxes have a high tax component in their social security systems. Countries with high payroll taxes also have high insurance components. Again there are exceptions to the rules as the aforementioned French social security contributions (CSG) show, since they are earmarked for social transfers. In addition, most welfare states have used various forms of discount factors – demographic, business-cycle adjustments or plainly redistributive ones – which lead to a varying degree of equivalence between contributions and benefits. All things considered, however, a welfare state that is based on ideal-type social security contributions should clearly have the highest degree of equivalence between taxes and social transfers.

Let us summarize the major points of this chapter. First, we have seen that tax and social policies are closely knit together. If we focus on taxes only, we might forget functional equivalents. For this reason I will return to these equivalents at a later stage. Second, we have seen that in the tax mix there is a remarkable shift away from income taxation. We have also seen that some countries such as Sweden or the US resisted this trend. Third, we have seen that the tax mix reveals underlying structural characteristics. Countries in which income taxation dominates have – on average – more inclusive and progressive tax systems as well as lower insurance components. With this information in mind, we can now turn to the effects these taxes have on the labour market.

NOTES

1. Translation: be-steuern – to steer 'to direct with a steer', stiuren 'to direct, lead, support, help, grant, endow, to pay a duty', stiuren 'to force into a direction, direct'. The etymological relationship between both German roots – contribution and steering wheel – remains unresolved so far (Seebold, 2002: 882).
2. Issues of democratic mobilization and taxation go back to the roots of early democracies

where 'taxation' meant 'representation'. Historically, it was the growing tax burden that made people demand specific prerogatives such as parliamentary control of budget decisions. In the contemporary literature on comparative political economy, this relationship has been turned upside down. The tax system and level is a consequence of the degree of representation of different electoral 'segments'. If, say, turnout is higher among poor voters, one would expect higher levels of taxation (Franzese, 2002; Roemer, 2001). The idea that representation causes taxation is pervasive and has influenced other areas such as the theory of democratization (Meltzer and Richard, 1991; Boix, 2003). While this notion is certainly not wrong it neglects the potential for reverse causality.

3. The Dutch finance ministry, for instance, claws back $6295 from a total of $24 717 of gross unemployment benefits. Net benefits are only slightly higher than for an equivalent recipient in Austria (Adema, 2001: 16).

4. An empirical proof would go beyond the scope of this book. For a crude test I have regressed Adema's data on hidden versus universalistic tax-based social policies on a measure of median voter preference for spending versus taxation (?). Controlling for the tax burden, I find the following results for 14 countries: The more a state taxes benefits, and the less it uses implicit social policies, the more popular is spending versus taxation (results available on request).

5. If one accounts for differences in taxation of benefits, and the size of tax cuts and similar instruments in the public budget, the rate of the social expenditure of the USA rises from 15.8 (gross) to 23.4 (net) per cent of GDP whereas it drops for Denmark from 35.9 (gross) to 27.5 (net) per cent.

6. Homburg (2003: 90) gives an example. The first tax rate of the 2004 German income tax schedule applied only to a short income range between 7000 and 13 000 euro per annum. This allows politicians to cut the first rate 'ostentatiously' without losing too much public revenue.

7. The Eurostat (2004), produces another effective tax measure, but its temporal and cross-country coverage is limited.

8. Serious deviations were found for Canada on consumption taxes, the Czech Republic on labour taxation, Netherlands on capital taxation, Portugal on labour taxation, and Switzerland also on labour taxation (Carey and Rabesona, 2002: 143).

9. I thank the authors for sharing their data with me.

10. See Carey and Rabesona (2002: 133) for a detailed description of their method. I split labour income in the two sources OECD '1000' and '2000' + '3000', and adjusted the respective tax bases.

11. The results are available on request.

12. There are many different approaches to the concepts of path dependency and hysteresis in social sciences (for example Pierson, 2004), but few of these ever talk about how to operationalize these phenomena on grounds of a quantitative, political economy approach. Though hysteresis and nonstationarity are not the same as path dependence they are clearly related concepts.

13. Some authors claim that the introduction of the CSG may even be interpreted as the beginning of path-switching from a Bismarckian to a Beveridge system of financing social protection (Kato, 2003: 105).

14. Among other things, countries differ to the extent with which tax filing is obligatory.

15. For the German debate see Bedau *et al.* (1998) who argues that the German VAT is by and large proportional.

16. A major problem with this materialistic perspective is, of course, that economic models do not ascribe utility to the act of saving, but characterize it as deferred consumption. If saving plays a role in the formation of status or social security, normative implications of indirect taxation may well be more in line with the typical gut reactions of many people: it favours saving relative to consumption and arguably benefits richer people more than the poor.

3.   The economics of taxing labour

The aim of this chapter is to investigate the role of the tax mix in the determination of employment and unemployment. It may come as a surprise that the answer is not immediately in the affirmative, but depends on the specific conditions under which a given labour market works. This chapter will therefore provide a survey of the theoretical and empirical economics literature on the link between taxation and (un-)employment.[1] It will apply the key insights in this literature to the question of the tax mix and will give some empirical evidence on an aggregate basis. The chapter will not only provide information about normative consequences – what is an optimal tax mix? – but it will also give an account of the economic tradeoffs and restrictions policy-makers face when choosing tax rates.

The first section describes the 'choice menu' of different theoretical approaches to unemployment, as selecting a particular approach already entails consequences for the link between taxation and the labour market. The second section deals with the overall problem of high total taxation and unemployment. As will become clear, the theories lead to contradictory answers once you allow for imperfectly functioning labour markets. The third section extends the survey to issues of the tax structure: progressivity, tax base, and the insurance component. The fourth section takes a closer look at empirical studies which have been performed on the impact of labour taxation. It will become clear that one of the crucial empirical issues is that the quantitative response of unemployment towards changes in tax policy is different in each country. Some simple regressions illustrate these problems, and show where to look for differences in the impact of the tax mix on labour markets. These findings substantiate the claim that some tax forms matter more than others, and that this insight especially holds true for sectors with lower productivity. The final section summarizes the chapter's major theoretical, empirical and normative findings.

INTRODUCTION: MODELS OF UNEMPLOYMENT

In the following I could never pretend to provide an adequate summary of all facets of economic approaches to the phenomenon of unemployment.

Readers with a good understanding of labour economics are well advised
to skip this section. However, a quick sketch of these approaches is inevi-
table since the state-of-the-art on the issue of labour taxation is divided
along many 'bifurcations' of different basic models for unemployment.
The choice of the model, as is to be shown, is decisive for evaluating the
employment effects of different tax forms. But before I deal with these different approaches a disclaimer seems appropriate.

General Disclaimer

A disclaimer has to be made for what follows. Most contemporary
approaches to either labour supply or unemployment, and their relationship to taxation, consist of partial micro-foundations for the aggregate
supply side of an economy. They admit that there is a certain level of cyclical or demand-side unemployment, but assume that the bulk of the tax
effect lies in the labour market itself. The flip-side of this implicit assumption is, of course, that these forms of unemployment can be easily differentiated from the form of stable 'structural' unemployment that is due to
supply-side factors. Such a distinction invites critique from many different
directions (Bluestone, 2001; Franz, 1993). In fact, most macroeconomists
would stress the role of both aggregate supply and demand shocks for the
evolution of unemployment rates across time (Layard *et al.*, 1991).

Moreover, most of the approaches that will be reviewed have also been
criticized for being 'partial partial analyses' (Atkinson, 1993: 23), in the
sense that they not only focus on the labour market, neglecting general
equilibrium effects, but also on work instead of welfare. Some labour
market experts (and politicians) argue that work itself has an intrinsic
value (ibid.). Correspondingly, I will focus on partial equilibrium models,
but give some hints when results may be changing because of aggregate
feedback effects. I will only analyse two out of the three major problems
identified by the OECD regarding the relationship between taxes and the
labour market (OECD, 1997b): taxes as an unemployment trap and as a
problem of increasing labour costs. Where adequate, however, I will also
briefly deal with the third, that is taxes as a poverty trap for the low wage
sector. This is of importance for cases when employment and welfare consequences of changes in tax policies diverge.

Having said this, there is substantial reason to believe that taxation has
the potential to affect (un-)employment through the aggregate supply side.
As is to be shown taxes are among the strong suspects for cross-country
variation and longer time periods. The aforementioned caveats obviously
limit the ability to make analytical and normative generalizations. The
focus on static versus dynamic issues, employment instead of welfare

and supply versus aggregate demand issues seems justified, I am more concerned with the reactions of politicians towards problems, and these are arguably stronger in the short run and in cases where policies directly affect employment.

A Quick Glance at Different Models

To understand how taxation influences (un-)employment, a quick primer in different economic explanations of labour market performance is necessary. It is necessary because channels, and ultimately, predictions differ dramatically between these approaches.

In the competitive model (CM) the labour market should behave as any other perfect market, that is it should clear. Firms are profit-maximizing entities, treat labour the same as as any other factor and take wages as given. They will hire workers as long as the marginal productivity of workers equals the (marginal) wage. Wages themselves are set competitively as a result of labour demand and supply. Workers balance their utility of working, that is receiving wages for consumption, and of not working, that is leisure and out-of-work income such as social transfers. Taxes create a difference between nominal wages and real purchasing power. The so-called tax wedge can, but need not have an impact on the input of labour. It is an empirical question depending on the responsiveness of supply and demand towards taxation. The usual hunch of the CM is that the prime effect of taxation lies in its potential to reduce employment. If unemployment occurs at all it is of frictional nature and arise as a consequence of transaction costs during the job search or as a consequence of structural barriers in the market causing mismatch between supply and demand.

Starting with the latter Mismatch Theory (MT) models a relationship between unemployment and a set of variables accounting for structural imbalances across economic sectors or social groups. *Prima facie*, these approaches merely provide a descriptive image of the situation, unless they are enriched by an explicit sociological or economic theory of structural barriers – for instance in the so-called theories of labour market segmentation. Alternatively, mismatch approaches recur to theories of the firm, of migration or of efficiency wages or wage bargaining (Layard *et al.*, 1991: 302). Mismatch theories provide an understanding of the problem of heterogeneity among the workforce. Though mismatch is a sectoral phenomenon of unemployment, it necessarily pushes up the overall level of unemployment (Layard *et al.*, 1991: 47).

Search Theories (ST) explain turnover and unemployment spells by focusing on the process of taking-up (inflow) and leaving jobs (outflow). The inflow rate depends on a set of factors exogenous to the theory, whereas the outflow rate depends on the number of vacancies and the search effectiveness of the individual (Layard *et al.*, 1991: 217). Search effectiveness may depend on many factors such as outside options of people who are not working or the individual characteristics of the unemployed. A major empirical merit of these approaches is that they give an account of the rising trend in long-term unemployment (Franz, 1993: Chapter 6). Feedback effects lead to a deteriorating search effectiveness across time in most European economies (Pissarides, 1992). Unlike in MT, unemployment leads to skill losses and hence leads to less productivity and output, which may have feedback effects on employment levels.

If taxes matter at all in simple models of MT and ST, then this is because they (a) affect different economic sectors differently, and (b) affect the search behaviour of individuals. These models explain why some people are more likely to become permanent outsiders, but the actual mechanism of how unemployment arises in the first place remains opaque. Efficiency-wage and wage-bargaining theories point at excessive real wages as the sources of unemployment. Variations of these two approaches have become the workhorses for many recent contributions to the analysis of unemployment and noncompetitive labour markets, and also play a prominent role in discussions of the issue of labour taxation.

An appropriate rationale for wages higher than in the CM is to assume that either firms or workers bid up wages. In the case of Efficiency-Wage Theories (EWT) it is the firms that push up wages in order to elicit their workers' productivity and effort. This may be the case if firms want to avoid workers quitting their jobs after they have invested in training, or because they have broader motivational aims. In the analysis of the consequences of taxation, it usually matters little which rationale makes firms push up wages (Goerke, 2002: 51). However, it is useful to stick to a particularly well-known version used by Shapiro and Stiglitz (1984). They argue that employees want to avoid working, 'shirking' in their terminology, and detection is costly for employers. In such a case, the firm has an incentive to pay wages above the market clearing level, so that effort responds positively to (net-of-tax) real wages.

Labour demand depends on the effort workers exert. Under standard assumptions for the production function of firms, labour demand increases with this effort. Workers trade off the disutility of increasing effort with the disutility of being caught in the act of shirking. The wage is higher than in standard cases where firms maximize profits by equating the marginal costs of labour – wages – with their marginal product. A particular feature of this theory is its recursive nature: eliciting workers' effort leads to higher wages and hence unemployment, but unemployment reduces workers' incentives to cheat. The rationale behind the latter fact is that without any unemployment workers would not have to fear the negative consequences of being caught. Unemployment is a disciplinary device, as it makes shirking more costly (Blanchard and Fischer, 1989: 460). In EWT taxation reduces the net wage of workers and therefore decreases workers' effort. In the short run the EWT is ambiguous about the normative implications of taxation, since employment and welfare effects could work in opposite directions. Yet, in the long run, assuming zero firm profits, tax and wage changes work in the same direction and lead to higher unemployment (Goerke, 2002: 59).

Efficiency wage models assume that firms set wages and employment levels. However, in many countries unions may exert an influence on wages by bargaining with employers (associations). Wage-Bargaining Theories (WBT) investigate the possibilities for unions rather than firms to bid up wages. As later chapters show WBT is most closely related to political economy accounts (Calmfors and Driffill, 1988; Iversen, 1999) so that I will dedicate some more time to their description. Approaches within the set of WBT differ in two crucial aspects: first, in the utility function of the unions; second in the structure of the wage bargaining (Oswald, 1982).

As for the former, older approaches mainly discuss whether unions follow a process of maximizing the utility of the pivotal mean or median member. Newer approaches endogenize union membership, since wage bargaining also has an impact on the incentive for individuals to join or not to join. In essence, the union has to overcome a problem of collective action, since wage increases often cover all workers whether they are members or not. These models include certain benefits such as a reputation effect, which is only available to union members. In its most general form the objective function of a utilitarian union may be denoted as (Goerke, 2002: 11)

$$Utility = n(v(w) + r^e) + \rho(l - n)v(R) \tag{3.1}$$

This is a weighted utility of those who are employed (n) – the first term of the RHS – and those that are unemployed ($l - n = u$). An employed person derives utility v from (net) wages and the reputation effect of being a member r^e. The unemployed benefits from the reservation wage R, usually some kind of a social benefit. If ρ, the degree of 'utilitarianess' of the union's objective, equals zero, then the union only represents employed people – the classic example of pure insider-ship.

Given the utility function of unions and the profit maximization of employers, the result of wage bargaining can be modelled by the Nash product between trade unions and employers' associations (see Equation 3.2). The Nash-product is a weighted distribution of gains from bargaining between the two sides. Since both sides have a reservation strategy, which is not to bargain, both sides must derive some net gains. Firms want to make a profit $\Pi \geq 0$, whereas unions maximize the difference between the wage w and the reservation wage R. The distribution, however, might be influenced by some β, a measure of bargaining power between employers and unions. If β is equal to one, we have a monopoly union dictating the bargaining, at the other extreme ($\beta = 0$) and the zero-profit condition ($\Pi = 0$) we obtain the result of the CM with zero rent for the union.

$$NP = [(1 - \rho)n(w - R)]^{\beta}(\Pi)^{1-\beta} \tag{3.2}$$

Thus, the specific form of this product depends on the kind of bargaining between employers and unions. In the case where a monopoly union faces many firms, the union can set both wages and employment levels. In the so-called Right-to-Management models (RTM) the union sets the wage unilaterally (as in the monopoly union case) or bargains over it, but the management decides on employment. In this case it is usually assumed that there are many unions and firms, and that taxes and transfers are given. There are other bargaining models (Oswald, 1993), but these are enough to show that the objectives of unions and the structure of bargaining matter for taxation. If, for instance, unions care about all employed people, then they are likely to include the general effects of taxation in their own calculations. Otherwise, the interests of insiders are more important and the issue depends on how taxation affects members relative to non-members. This effect interacts with the bargaining structure. In RTM the union only bargains on wages and the tax effect will be larger than in models of a monopoly union which also determines employment. If taxation also affects union membership the tax effect could almost vanish, but it is difficult to yield general predictions (see below).

As mentioned in the disclaimer, all these models share a number of problematic assumptions about the role of aggregate demand, firms as price-takers or the importance of welfare state institutions (Layard *et al.*, 1991: Chapter 7). On empirical grounds it is obvious that none of the different approaches emerges as the best explanation for unemployment (Layard *et al.*, 1991; Bean, 1994). Yet unemployment shows some persistence, though not necessarily perfect 'hysteresis', and is therefore, by and large, in line with a broad notion of insider-outsider models (Heijdra and Ploeg, 2002: 205). The fact that persistence in some countries is much smaller than in others adds plausibility to the claim that the institutional structures of labour markets have a deep impact. Given this ambiguity it is probably best to elaborate the tax effect on employment with a comparison of different models – predominantly EWT and WBT. This is what the next two sections intend to do.

TAX BURDEN AND LABOUR MARKETS

To understand the effects of a revenue-neutral shift in the tax structure, we need to know first the employment effects of the tax burden. The empirical evidence on aggregate labour supply is very mixed, since different groups in the population respond differently to changes in tax parameters (Blundell and MaCurdy, 1999), but also because countries are so different (Alesina *et al.*, 2005). Findings in the literature are bewildering. Nickell and Layard (1999: 3037) argue that taxes do not play an empirical role in long-run unemployment, and could only matter theoretically under 'peculiar' circumstances.[2] Other authors find an impact both on a theoretical (Goerke, 2002) and an empirical (Daveri and Tabellini, 2000) basis. OECD publications are particularly ambivalent. In 1995 the OECD argued (p. 14) that it is specific features of the tax system, rather than the tax burden, which cause wage pressure and unemployment, only to reach the opposite conclusion two years later (OECD, 1997b: 68): 'Tax burden must not just be shifted from one form of labour tax to another but the tax burden on labour must be cut.' After reviewing 20 studies on the impact of taxation on unemployment, Fuest (2000) finds a majority (13) arguing for and a minority (7) arguing against the importance of the tax burden. It is intriguing to investigate the origins of these differences.

Competitive Markets and Labour Supply

In labour markets where structural unemployment is absent, the major channel to investigate is the effect of taxation on employment, and on labour supply in particular.[3] The basic microeconomic framework for an analysis of the incidence of taxation says that taxation leads, *ceteris paribus*, to a substitution effect: work is either replaced by more leisure, by other sources of income, or by an increased amount of work in the future (Gustafsson, 1996: 822). Taxation may also lead to capital-intensive production, informal employment (Schneider, 2002), or a substitution towards household production and work (for example Esping-Andersen, 1999). The main causal mechanism for all these processes is a 'wedge' between gross and net wages. Yet a lower net wage only leads to smaller labour supply, if the substitution effect of taxation dominates the income effect. This depends on the alternative out-of-work income a person can generate and on the characteristics of the individual.

The shift between consumption and leisure can either be modelled as a yes-or-no decision whether to participate or a decision about how many hours someone wants to work. If, however, the decision on working hours depends on collective bargaining between trade unions and employers it does not necessarily reflect the individuals' preferences (Blundell, 1995: 10). Other factors can make the prediction of employment on changes in taxes and wages even more difficult. For example, the decision to work carries fixed costs for the individual, which differ between countries. Among these child-care costs are noteworthy as they are much higher in continental Europe than in North America or Scandinavia (Esping-Andersen, 1999: 66). Moreover, tax and transfer systems shape the functional form of budget constraints in a non-linear fashion. Under such circumstances, what may lead to lower employment in some parts of the income spectrum may lead to opposite results in adjacent regions. National income tax regimes differ in terms of progressiveness and the number of tax 'kinks', both of which dilute the explanatory power of average tax rates in international comparisons (Nickell and Layard, 1999: 3037). Similarly, different national treatments of joint taxation for married couples make comparisons truly intricate. If Sweden, for instance, was to apply the German system of joint income taxation, female labour force participation would drop from 80 to 60 per cent (Gustafsson, 1996: 833).

Microeconometric studies on labour supply have shown that for some social groups such as single mothers, the income effect surpasses the substitution effect (Blundell, 1995). In those cases labour supply is backward bending, that is decreasing in net wages. Opposite results hold for housewives who withdraw from the labour market relatively quickly in response to increases in taxation and accompanying decreases of real wages (Blundell and MaCurdy, 1999: 1645). We can expect an intermediate result on an aggregate level for whole sectors of an economy or even for the entire labour market. In other words, labour supply responds to taxation in the classic fashion, although the total effect is usually small in micro-studies. In particular, differences are large between different segments of the income/wage spectrum. Low-wage work is typically found to be highly inelastic to both wages and taxation (Borjas, 2004), but this finding does not hold for all countries in the same way (Blundell and MaCurdy, 1999). Alesina *et al.* (2005) show that the macro-evidence for an impact of taxation on employment is much stronger and hence clashes with the evidence on this micro level. One way to explain this puzzle lies in the assumption of 'social multipliers', that is people have stronger preferences for leisure, if everybody else does. If these effects are present micro-evidence underestimates labour supply responses.

Non-competitive Markets and Unemployment

The question of whether the tax burden has an impact on unemployment can be approached in two steps: first, do taxes increase pressure on wages to go up; second, do higher wages lead to higher labour costs, which firms are unable to roll-over?

As for the first issue – taxes and wage increases – simple versions of ST, EWT and WBT models provide a similar rationale. If both wages and the reservation income are equally taxed, changes in the tax parameters will not change unemployment rates (Pissarides, 1998). To take one example Layard *et al.* (1991: 108) show the irrelevance of taxation for the case of union bargaining with unemployment benefits as the only available reservation wage. In their model, benefits are a fixed proportion of net-of-tax wages, that is with tax parameters changing wages and reservation wages change equally $R = (1 - \tau)B$. In this case, the Nash product (see Equation 3.2) becomes

$$\Omega' = [w_i(1 - \tau) - B(1 - \tau)]^\beta S_i^\beta \Pi_i^e \tag{3.3}$$

Optimizing this Nickell and Layard (1999) yield the following result:

$$\frac{w_i(1 - \tau)}{w_i(1 - \tau) - B(1 - \tau)} = \frac{\beta \eta s_\pi + (1 - s_\pi)}{s_\pi} \tag{3.4}$$

Here, S_i represents the ratio of labour to capital input in production, whereas s_Π is the proportion of profits in value added. η is the wage elasticity of demand for labour, that is how labour demand responds to marginal changes in wages. s_Π and η act as weights for the distribution of the Nash product in addition to the bargaining power β. Since on the LHS of Equation 3.4 $(1 - \tau)$ may be cancelled out, optimization leads to a first-order condition independent of τ and equilibrium unemployment is unaffected.

This is a very stylized version of a reservation wage, since it abstracts from informal or capital income, and in our context most crucially, from other forms of welfare state transfers. For the low-wage sector, the reservation wage might be much more akin to a basic means tested social assistance. For people with higher skills transfers for housing, children or education are frequently excluded from taxation. In both cases there is no clear relationship between T and B, that is there is redistribution. Let's assume that R depends of two forms of transfers, one of which is untaxed (B_0):

$$R = B_0 + (1 - \tau) B_1 \tag{3.5}$$

Under such circumstances the terms including taxation of Equation 3.4 do not cancel out, and taxes raise unemployment, since they change the relative proportion between wages and reservation wage (see Appendix). As trivial as this example may seem, it is not innocuous, since it implies that any social security system with a certain degree of redistribution induces a form of incentive problem through high levels of taxation. Stiglitz (1999) reaches a similar conclusion using an efficiency wage explanation of unemployment. In general, Pissarides (1998) shows that such a result holds for a variety of different models, including search, bargaining and efficiency wage models.

Of course this model is still crude. In the case of a utilitarian union, for example, Oswald (1982: 566) shows that the unambiguous effect of taxes on unemployment only holds for a sufficiently high elasticity of labour demand, for no other unearned income and for workers with relative risk aversion. At least for low-wage workers, there is good reason to believe that these assumptions hold and that taxation has an impact on unemployment for non-competitive labour markets with a system of redistributive social transfers.

To know whether this effect is not only a necessary but also sufficient explanation of higher unemployment, one has to know whether firms themselves are facing higher labour costs because of increasing taxation. This question has created a cottage industry for empirical analyses on labour demand and the incidence of taxation (OECD, 1990; Hamermesh, 1993). The basic insight of this research tradition is that no matter which market side is officially taxed, the burden itself falls on the market side with fewer 'exit options', or in technical terms: a lower elasticity (Homburg, 2003: 155). As with the question of labour supply, the question of the incidence of taxation is hence an empirical one. Hamermesh (1993), having reviewed numerous studies on labour demand, concludes that demand elasticities are typically positive,[4] whereas elasticities of labour supply are much smaller (see previous section). Correspondingly, in the long run most of the burden falls on workers, either through lower nominal wages for given prices, or through lower real wages as a consequence of higher prices.[5] This shows that the focus on these three tax forms (see Chapter 2) is justified. Yet, shifting never works perfectly, not even in the long run. Both Hamermesh (1993) and the OECD (1990) conclude in their surveys that some 60 to 70 per cent of taxes are typically shifted towards workers, though in some studies shifting may indeed be higher.[6]

Finally, there are some factors that make shifting more complicated. First of all, in a EWT model the shifting of taxation does not work perfectly (OECD, 1990: 154), since taxes reduce effort and firms may even be induced – via higher taxation – to pay higher wages. Shifting might not work if there are other labour market institutions, such as a minimum wage or a basic income scheme. Finally, shifting the tax burden might be entirely different for different segments of the workforce. Workers with highly specialized human capital may respond totally elastically, and therefore the task of bearing the brunt of the burden remains with employers (Homburg, 2003: 131). Similarly the low-wage sector may be too close to the reservation wage to be given a major share of the burden (Scharpf, 1999).[7] Most importantly, differences in shifting the burden of taxation may also be due to differences in the structure of taxation (OECD, 1990). Hence, it is now time to proceed to the core interest of this book: the tax structure.

TAX STRUCTURE AND LABOUR MARKETS

The last section has confirmed the conjecture that the major part of contemporary tax forms – and income, payroll, and indirect taxation in particular – fall on wages, that is labour. It has also argued that under many different theoretical settings, the tax burden itself enhances unemployment, but that this effect is clearly conditional on other factors such as a redistributive social transfer system. Moreover, it gave reason to believe that pure tax burden effects are becoming ambiguous once differences of tax structure are accounted for.

With unemployment remaining unabated at high levels in some countries, the quest for an optimal design of the tax system has aroused fresh attention from scholars. Fuest (2000) argues that a change from payroll towards indirect taxation might be beneficial for employment given the broader base of the latter. Heijdra and Ploeg (2002: 206) say that there is substantive theoretical or empirical reason to believe that unemployment may actually fall with the progression of income taxes. Finally, some evidence (Disney, 2004), shows that the insurance function of payroll taxes mitigates the distortive impact of taxation on employment. Policy-makers are left in a cyclical situation, where no clear winner emerges. This section, therefore, delves into the consequences of tax structure in more detail. We will discuss how the tax base, tax progression and its insurance component affect the labour market.

Tax Base and Participation

One of the key insights of optimal tax theories is that the broader the tax base, the better the outcome in terms of welfare for all (for example Homburg, 2003). This is due to the fact that if different factors of production or different forms of economic behaviour are taxed equally there is less potential for evasive action and hence for economic distortions. Since disincentives for work are a major form of distortion, employment effects, in general, tend to follow welfare effects. Therefore, tax-cut-cum base broadening – in a competitive market setting – should also be an

employment-friendly policy. We will first make a brief detour to first-best
tax systems and the difference between capital and labour taxation. Then
we go on to policy proposals that either deal with exempting specific (low-
wage) sectors or with shifting taxes from one form to the other.

A thorough discussion of the different principles for taxing income would
go beyond our present needs. To give but one example: Governments
across the world tend to tax both corporate profits and capital income,
a practice criticized by some economists. Many scholars argue that pure
expenditure taxes are better than income tax systems, although they may
not cover all forms of income, and consequently have a narrower base (see
Rose quoted in Homburg (2003: 173)). If, however, such a revenue-neutral
change from income to expenditure taxation means an increasing burden
for labour, the welfare effects of such a tax reform remain ambiguous
(Homburg, 2003: 209). More importantly, expenditure taxes have rarely
been implemented, and whenever this was tried it proved to be a short-lived
political experiment (Ganghof, 2006). For whatever reason, first-best tax
systems are hard to implement.[8] A general consumption tax such as a VAT
treats all forms of consumption, and hence implicitly all forms of factor
income, equally. Such a tax policy is the closest approximation of a first-
best tax system of expenditure taxes. Empirically, the tax base of a VAT is
broader than that of a payroll and income tax (see Chapter 2). This should
make general consumption taxes 'employment-friendly'.

Without a first-best tax system, a key question of how to tax income is
whether 'capital' or 'labour' should be taxed. In recent years, the 'political
discursive cycle' on the debate between capital versus labour taxation has
arguably declined. Whether it is the high liquidity of (financial) capital, and
the globalization of capital markets or pernicious effect on investments and
growth, the taxation of capital income has become 'unfashionable' among
economists these days. Only under very specific circumstances, it may be
attractive to switch tax bases from labour to capital. Fuest (2000: 33), for
instance, shows that such a switch can enhance employment in cases where
labour taxes are higher than taxes on capital and where governments cannot
tax profits. The latter assumption is not far from the observation that tran-
snational companies do have the capacity to avoid the taxation of profits
(Ganghof, 2000). However, if capital taxation is completely rolled over on
wages, as Nickell (1997) argues, the employment effects vanish.[9] In short,
shifting the mix towards capital can be a difficult enterprise for politicians.

If a first-best tax system is not feasible, one has to look for second-best
taxes that follow the rule of inverse elasticities: they put the highest burden
on those sources with the lowest capacity for evasion. This implies that
even in terms of employment it seems to be beneficial to tax labour, if
capital is too sensitive. Neglecting minor forms of taxation one is hence left

with a dilemma: how to reduce the tax burden on labour without reducing the overall burden. An important way lies in excluding specific segments of the labour market rather than all workers.

The case for the implicit subsidization of low-wage labour is worth considering. This sector seems to be particularly sensitive to taxation, due to the range of factors discussed on pp. 31–2. In particular, if low-wage workers have outside options, tax deductions may lure them into the labour market again. Basic allowances are also important in this respect and may not only have equity, but also employment effects. The conjecture that exempting the low-wage sector always leads to higher employment must however be rejected. As in the case of tax-based employment subsidies or tax credits many authors have shown that such policy tools usually have ambiguous effects on employment (Borjas, 2004: 619). And yet it is important to note that in non-competitive labour markets tax policy implications diverge from those of the competitive case. If unemployment is concentrated on specific groups, broadening the base can lead to higher taxation in these segments and to less employment (Scharpf, 2000). Let us therefore specify more closely under what theoretical assumptions a shift from one tax form to another can improve the performance of labour markets.

To compare the employment effects of different tax forms, one needs to look at the differences between the effects of average tax rates for income, payroll and indirect taxes on employment. Unfortunately, not all unemployment models deliver the same results – indeed, most of them deliver outcomes that are ambiguous. As is the case with the tax burden, for income taxes the crucial assumption is whether R is taxed. If so, unemployment rises with the burden and falls with the level of tax exemption (Goerke, 2002: 81) in WBT models. In particular, income taxation can act as a second-best policy option, if political or economic reasons forbid the removal of distortions as a first-best scenario. Chang *et al.* (1999), for instance, find evidence that a shift away from indirect towards direct (income) taxation can enhance employment, if a VAT cannot be shifted forward.

The case for a switch from payroll taxes is also not without ambiguity. In a union bargaining model, a rise in the tax level can reduce unemployment, since the Nash product of bargaining shrinks and, for bargaining to remain profitable for both sides, unions must accept lower wages. But again, this effect is not robust against an alternative model set-up, such as endogenous membership (Goerke, 2002: 161). The level of payroll taxes is ambiguous in EWT models only in the short run, whereas it increases unemployment in the long run (ibid.: 179). This is so because firms are in the short run unwilling to reduce wages for fear of a decrease in workers' efforts. In the long run, these firms are driven out of the market and wages increase, as does unemployment.

Even if general consumption taxes have the largest tax base, their effects are hard to predict in models with unemployment (Goerke, 2002: 202), since they not only depend on the question whether the reservation wage is taxed, but also on whether firms actually manage to shift taxes on to prices. If no shift occurs, a VAT is equivalent to payroll taxes in its employment effects, if full shifting occurs it is akin to (proportional) income taxes. With a certain degree of shifting the question of whether VAT is harmful is an empirical one. For the case of EWT Goerke (2002: 259) states that a switch from payroll to general indirect taxes is only beneficial for employment if benefits are not indexed to inflation. For the case of an open economy, it has been argued that tax competition is smaller for indirect taxes than for income or payroll taxes, if consumption is taxed where it occurs (Homburg, 2003). This is usually the most forceful argument for shifting the basis towards indirect taxation (Kato, 2003). If, however, consumption itself is mobile or elastic, for instance if it disappears into the shadow economy, the case for indirect taxes as a response to international competition loses some of its lustre.

One might also propose a final reform scenario: from payroll to income taxation. In fact, Atkinson (1995) shows for the case of a segmented labour market and a ST framework that such a switch is beneficial due to its tax base effects. Goerke (2002) reaches a similar conclusion via another explanation. Since the reservation wage is either not taxed or is only taxed as far as employees' social security contributions and income taxes are concerned, a shift from employers' to employees' taxation decreases unemployment. In this sense Goerke rejects the old 'Invariance of Incidence Proposition' according to which it does not matter whether formally workers or employers have to pay the taxes.

All things considered, the case for indirect taxation as the best tax form for employment is strong on the basis of efficiency considerations, in particular in an open economy, but is less so in a non-competitive labour market. The possibility of exempting sensitive sectors such as the low-wage sector may prompt calls for a tax mix based on income taxes with high basic allowances. It remains an empirical question whether this effect will dominate the general tax base effect. If indirect taxes are indeed employment-efficient, we are once again in the traditional efficiency versus redistribution tradeoff.

Progressivity and Redistribution

How does progressivity affect an imperfect labour market? Van der Ploeg, for instance, argues that 'In a second-best world the distortions arising from non-competitive labour markets are partially offset by the distortions arising from progressive taxes' (quoted in Goerke, 2002: 115). This is no new insight, since tax-based income policies have been known about for quite some time (Wallich and Weintraub, 1971). If we are interested not so much in curbing inflation, but in labour market outcomes, it is still a controversial question as to how far progression directly affects unemployment. Stiglitz (1999), for instance, argues that disincentives arise not from tax progression per se, but from the more general desire to redistribute. It is also important to note that in CM models employment falls with both average and marginal tax rates (for example Fuest, 2000: 72).

The more benign perspective on tax progression is easy to understand for WBT. Tax progression makes wage pressure at the margin less attractive to unions. The more a union tries to bid up wages, the more it gets punished by tax progression. Goerke, for instance, finds that a revenue-neutral rise in marginal rates holds for a large variety of WBT models. A positive relationship between employment and marginal tax rates is also shown for the case of small open economies where trade unions compete with each other internationally (Koskela and Holm, 1995). This is the case since unions now factor in the responses of their counterparts in other countries. The effects are ambiguous in EWT models, since progressivity also decreases employers' ability to elicit effort from workers.

There are a number of theoretical criticisms of this understanding of progression. First, Fuest (2000) shows that if bargaining takes place not only on wages but also on working hours, the positive effect of progression on employment vanishes. Rather, higher marginal rates lead to less working hours. The specific utility function of the union then determines whether there is a negative or positive employment effect. Second, higher marginal rates may lead to disincentives in other areas, namely the accumulation of human capital (Fuest, 2000). In these cases marginal rates decrease employment and increase unemployment.[10] If tax progression also shows a negative impact, a logical step is to conceptualize the issue as an optimal degree of tax progression which balances the good effects on wage restraint with the bad effects on worker productivity. For 'realistic' calibrations such an optimal progression may be comparatively high in non-competitive labour markets (Sørensen, 1999).

Let's take a closer look at the empirical literature for information about the level of this optimal progressivity. A number of studies corroborate the claim of Van der Ploeg, such as Lockwood and Manning (1993) for the UK, Schneider (2004) for Germany or Hutton and Ruocco (1999) for simulation models for four continental European countries. Studies on Norway (Aaberge *et al.*, 1995) and Denmark (Hansen *et al.*, 2000) show more ambivalent results. In particular, Hansen *et al.* (2000) show that the results may sway empirically between the predictions for a competitive market exemplified by white collar workers and those for a non-competitive market such as the one for organized blue collar workers. This is also consistent with the findings of Disney's (2000) survey. He argues that labour supply, and unemployment, depends on marginal rates in four instances: for low income workers if progression interacts with social benefits; for high income earners if marginal rates reduce effort and investment in human capital; for older workers if it increases the probability of them retiring early; and for younger workers if it makes their entry into the labour market more difficult.

All things considered, the balance of evidence seems to be tilted towards advocates of tax progression. Of course, liberal economists will always argue that it is better to remove the sources of the distortion rather than trying to minimize its costs.[11] Moreover, the theoretical debate could surely spin the wheel of policy advice, once worker heterogeneity and long run general equilibrium effects have been accounted for. Nevertheless, the finding that progression and employment are reconcilable seems to bolster the case of scholars who argue the case for different institutional systems achieving similar employment outcomes. In this respect it is important to note that progression does not only imply redistribution, but also insurance (Sinn, 1995).

Insurance and Contingency

Most forms of taxation entail – explicitly or implicitly – an insurance component. This is most obvious in the case of payroll taxes defined as 'tax2000' in the OECD revenue statistics including social security contributions (see Chapter 2). This contradicts the narrow definition of the term 'taxation'. The tendency to fuse the border between taxes and earmarked contributions has led to an overly negative perception of payroll taxes (Disney, 2004). But even Disney's conception of the insurance component of taxation is only part of the picture, since any kind of tax-based redistribution – be it in the form of progression or in the form of flat benefits and proportional taxes – leads to insurance for people whose income is uncertain. Hence the debate on tax-based insurance has two dimensions. First, a narrow one focusing on earmarked taxes; second, a broader one on the welfare implications of taxation which holds for all major forms of taxation, as long as there is an element of redistribution attached to it.

Starting with the first, Disney (2004) shows that the negative impact of payroll taxes decreases considerably if payroll taxes are divided into an insurance and a tax component, that is those contributions for which there is no adequate contingent claim on social transfers or in-kind benefits. He finds that more women seek employment when the insurance component of social security contributions is higher. For male workers and the low-wage sector his findings resemble the overall picture of labour supply discussed earlier: there is hardly any aggregate effect visible at all (ibid.: 298). This empirical evidence counteracts the poor image of payroll taxes developed in previous sections. Since it is social security contributions that – by definition – are most closely related to benefits (see Chapter 2), the employment effects of these taxes should be lower compared with those of both income and indirect taxes.

Sinn (1995) broadens the insurance character of taxation to include all major forms. Specifically, he argues that public insurance via redistribution can enhance welfare. Welfare states not only provide a safety net (workers feel better, if you will), but they also encourage workers to engage in riskier activities. This public provision of insurance can be socially optimal under certain assumptions. Most fundamentally, workers have to be risk-averse, that is they have to be insurance-seekers (Agell, 2002). If so, well-known problems of market failures in markets with asymmetric information can justify the public provision of social insurance.

The implications for the discussion on employment are twofold. First, if tax-based redistribution enlarges the pie of consumption possibilities, it reduces some of the tax burden effects found on pp. 31–2. Second, different tax forms differ in their effects on welfare and consequently on employment. Since income and payroll taxation harms private efforts of self-insurance – for example by impeding major investments in human capital – risk-taking may overshoot and welfare and employment dip downward relative to the social optimum (Sinn, 1995: 512). *Ceteris paribus*, taxes on cash flows and on consumption are less distorting for self-insurance activities and are therefore better for employment (Sinn, 1995: 515). One may also generalize this argument for the case of low-wage earners. For low-wage earners the insurance function of taxation comes, by and large, in Sinn's notion of redistribution rather than in Disney's notion of forced savings. This implies that a welfare state financed by proportional payroll taxation is less beneficial for low-wage earners than one that is financed out of general income or indirect taxation.

Unfortunately, dealing with the 'conservative core' of the welfare state, that is its capacity to take care of contingency, makes the issue of taxation and employment much more complex in two ways. A first problem is that the move from a world of perfect information to uncertainty automatically leads to the question of how beliefs about different states of the world are formed. The most prominent example is fiscal illusion and visibility (see Chapter 4). A second major problem with insurance is collective action. Such a failure not only haunts markets but also governments. Since no government has perfect oversight over the nature of contingencies, people will find ways of maximizing their payoffs from insurance schemes by either contributing less, or receiving benefits worth more than their actuarially fair value. The massive trend of early retirement might be read as such a problem of enforcement (Ebbinghaus, 2002). The crucial problem of a public insurance system is therefore that it could undermine itself and with it its employment-friendliness.

Moreover, the insurance issue is truly at the heart of much confusion about welfare state effects and, more specifically, the debate about labour market institutions. The question of whether it is rent or insurance seeking that explains the origins and the maintenance of these institutions, is hard to answer without any prior knowledge (Agell, 2002). One needs to impose more restrictive assumptions about the preferences and the behaviour of people to derive normative conclusions about the effects of institutions. Given these caveats it is difficult to directly compare the insurance effects of income, payroll and indirect taxes. *Prima facie*, payroll taxes are attractive for enhancing employment if they guarantee social benefits. Income taxes also provide some insurance because of their progressiveness. Insurance effects should be smaller for indirect taxes only, but all these claims are contingent on how they interact with the system of social expenditures and the willingness to invest in human capital.

I have completed the observations on the role of the tax mix in labour markets and found instances in which any of the three tax forms may emerge as a winner. We have seen, however, that tax progressivity is not incompatible with low-wage employment. To the contrary, direct progressivity alleviates the tax burden on low-wage earners whereas indirect progressivity exempts income below a certain threshold and thereby shows that it is not always a larger tax base which is employment-friendly. Insurance, finally, legitimizes the use of social security contributions, but, again, this is of less interest for low-wage earners who need insurance via redistribution. Taken together, it implies that of all three major forms of taxation, income taxes are the least detrimental for (low-wage) employment. This is an important hypothesis I will investigate empirically in the following.

EMPIRICS

Cross-country studies on the impact of taxation on employment have a major benefit: they account for effects not visible on the micro level. The major downside of aggregate analysis is that there are huge methodological problems in such comparisons. This section first addresses these particular problems in the hope of improving our understanding of why there is so much diversity in the empirical findings. Against this methodological background, I test the impact of the tax mix on both employment and unemployment. Obviously, I do not want to 'reinvent the wheel', since so many studies have already been done. But three issues mentioned above have received inadequate attention in most of these studies: differences in the impact of income, payroll and indirect taxation; the conditionality of findings on country-specific effects; and their particular relevance for low-wage sectors.

Methodological Problems in Empirical Studies

Some recent empirical studies based on international comparisons and the use of aggregate data reveal a puzzling diversity. Some authors (Daveri and Tabellini, 2000; Volkerink *et al.*, 2002) find that if the tax mix matters, payroll taxes are most problematic, while consumption taxes are generally considered to be less harmful, and income taxes range somewhere in between (OECD, 1995: 69). For others (Nickell, 1997; Disney, 2000; Hutton and Ruocco, 1999) the mix either does not matter or matters differently. In fact, there is a remarkable range of different findings that create too much ambivalence for useful policy recommendations. The question that arises is why this is the case. Daveri (2001) mentions three problems prevalent in all empirical studies – omitted variable bias, aggregation, endogeneity – to which I will add a fourth: poolability. I will briefly discuss each of them.

To begin with omitted variable bias, complex issues such as the connection between taxation and unemployment always create problems of model specification. If important variables are left out, taxes may load high simply because of their correlation with other variables (Disney, 2000). Yet, truly exogenous variables and correctly specified models would need more theoretical input. For example, one may include indicators for individuals' preferences for public spending. Some scholars have tried to correct for omitted variables and to account for endogeneity by the use of such instruments (for example Kato, 2003). It is likely that these variables are endogenous to taxation. Such approaches neither do justice to the problem of complementarities between certain types of public institutions, nor do they give a thorough account of the intricate relationships between taxes and indicators of spending. Other instruments may simply be inadequate. Empirical instruments such as government partisanship are well known in the comparative politics literature, but are not very good proxies for, say, government expenditure (Kittel and Obinger, 2003). Given these problems it is probably best not to exaggerate the fear of omissions.

The second problem of aggregation, is perhaps the most mundane, but certainly not the most trivial. Empirical problems of aggregation loom large in all studies, as already discussed in the previous sections. Even if studies were to find non-significant coefficients for tax parameters, this is not sufficient proof for the non-existence of causal relationships. Rather, as shown on pp. 35–42, the three dimensions of tax structure neutralize the aggregate impact of one tax form on employment (Nickell and Layard, 1999; Belot and van Ours, 2000). Bean (1994: 615) concludes that 'there is simply not enough information in the data to give clear signals on the relative merits of the competing hypotheses'. I think this statement is overly harsh. To the contrary, Alesina *et al.* (2005) have shown that micro- and macro-level analyses are important complementary tools for the evaluation of the tax effects on employment.

Nevertheless, econometric problems of pooling across countries and time are huge (Baltagi, 2005; Kittel and Winner, 2005). One source of predicament is the inclusion of institutional indicators. If these indicators do not vary across time, their effects are difficult to observe. If there are 'time-variant institutional' indicators (Iversen, 1999; Kenworthy, 2001) – the very term emits a somewhat paradoxical tone – they do so only limitedly. But even if we had a good and temporally varying indicator of an institution, institutional impacts across countries still matter because of institutional complementarities and the lack of random sampling in country-level analyses.

Since institutional indictors will never account for all country-specific effects, the question remains how to deal with these country effects while allowing for institutional variables. Scholars have looked for group specific effects in their approaches to this topic. Daveri and Tabellini (2000), for instance, group countries into three empirical clusters in a similar way as suggested by Esping-Andersen (1990). They find corroborative evidence that labour taxes matter more in continental European countries than in Scandinavia or the Anglo-Saxon world. What they do not show, however, is whether these effects are not, in fact, merely hidden country effects. More troublesome is the fact that such country groups have a dubious normative and theoretical status.[12] Many studies have ascribed country clusters the logical status of independent or intervening variables, whereas they are, at best, spherical ones (Kemmerling, 2003), that is regime types contain both dependent and independent variables.

The last problem to be discussed is endogeneity. It is obvious that the tax structure also depends on the performance of the labour market. With high levels of unemployment, tax revenues should decrease but 'demand' for taxes necessarily rises. Some authors (for example Iversen and Cusack, 2000) have tried to avoid this problem by distinguishing between discretionary and automatic changes in public budgets, but the issue at stake is more fundamental: there are theoretical reasons to believe that causal channels run in both directions and taxation and unemployment feed each other. Summers *et al.* (1992), for example, argue that the distortional impact of taxation on labour markets is lower in coordinated economies. If this premise is correct, politicians in these countries can raise taxes to a higher level than in other economies, since the optimal tax rate in terms of employment consequences is higher. There is, according to Daveri (2001), no easy way out of this problem, but there are some possibilities one of which is to endogenize politics in theory (see Chapter 4).

Simple Estimates of Tax Mixes and Employment

Given the previously discussed set of methodological problems, I have to be very cautious when conducting statistical inferences for aggregate data on taxation and employment. The method used here is therefore akin to Kittel and Obinger's (2003) step-by-step procedure when they analysed the link between economic integration and social expenditure. I begin this subsection with an analysis of the time-series and cross-section properties of the tax-employment relationship. In the following subsection I estimate pooled data. For all estimations I use three different labour market indicators: aggregate (business sector) employment rates, sectoral employment rates and rates of unemployment. All three indicators stem from the OECD, but the sectoral rates merit some elaboration. These rates are generated for each sector as total employment divided by the working age population. Three sectors have been singled out for their marked differences in skill levels: 'manufacturing', 'trade and hotels', and 'personal and social services'. Using information on sectoral productivity levels, workers in 'manufacturing' (ISIC3)[13] belong to the highly qualified part of the workforce, whereas workers in 'trade and hotels' (ISIC6) and 'personal and social services' (ISIC9) exhibit markedly lower skill inputs.[14]

Time-series results

A first step in analysing the tax employment link is to look at individual time series for selected countries. For the sake of simplicity, the analysis will focus on the three 'role models' in comparative welfare state analysis: Germany, Sweden and the US. These countries have been used before for comparative purposes given their well-known institutional differences (Blundell and MaCurdy, 1999; Esping-Andersen, 1990). Table 3.1 shows three models for the time series of rate of private sector employment. The model includes a lagged dependent variable and two independent variables to control for differences in the evolution of the labour markets: unemployment and wages. More importantly, the models contain the three major

Table 3.1   Time-series results for three countries

	Business sector employment to working-age population		
	GER	SWE	US
Intercept	40.573***	38.682***	6.921
	(8.109)	(5.925)	(12.385)
Lagged dependent	0.489***	0.397***	0.806***
	(0.100)	(0.092)	(0.209)
Unemployment	−0.853***	−0.885***	−0.939***
	(0.066)	(0.104)	(0.067)
Lag unemployment	0.310*	−0.002	0.714***
	(0.139)	(0.175)	(0.179)
Wage	0.135	−0.012	0.043
	(0.086)	(0.014)	(0.189)
Lag wage	0.073	0.021	−0.062
	(0.097)	(0.015)	(0.193)
Income taxes	0.107	0.037	0.113
	(0.101)	(0.044)	(0.094)
Lag income taxes	0.056	0.154**	0.034
	(0.101)	(0.056)	(0.105)
Payroll taxes	0.064	−0.092	0.332
	(0.247)	(0.054)	(0.408)
Lag payroll taxes	−0.811***	−0.158***	0.507
	(0.251)	(0.051)	(0.407)
Indirect taxes	−0.197	−0.481***	−0.146*
	(0.178)	(0.087)	(0.079)
Lag indirect taxes	−0.279	0.083	0.011
	(0.181)	(0.081)	(0.458)
Adj. R^2	1.000	0.998	0.998
Nobs.	27	27	27
F-Test restricted versus full (6, 15)	4.5***	8.75***	1.25
DW-h	−1.16	−1.235	−2.558***
ADF-Test (Intercept, Trend)	−2.771	−3.399***	−4.101***
	(1,1)	(−, −)	(1, −)

Notes:
Levels of significance: * < 0.10, ** < 0.05, *** < 0.01.
F-Test compares models with and without tax regressors.
DW-h: Durbin-Watson h-statistic for autocorrelation in AR-models.
ADF-Test: Augmented Dickey-Fuller test for nonstationarity. Parentheses indicate where inclusion of trend or intercept was necessary.

forms of taxation. All exogenous variables enter in contemporaneous levels and first temporal lags to allow for some endogeneity.

Table 3.1 shows pronounced differences in the tax coefficients. The tax variables exhibit a considerable variation across countries, although the overall effect in all three regressions is rather limited. In the case of the US, only indirect taxation has a weakly negative impact on private employment. Taken together, the tax variables do not seem to drive private employment in the US as the F-test statistics show.[15] Sweden is an opposite case to that of the US. Taxation adds to the explanatory power of the model. More interestingly, coefficients for payroll and indirect taxation are negative, whereas income taxation enters with a positive coefficient. For indirect taxation, it is the contemporaneous level which matters in Sweden, whereas it is the lagged level in the case of payroll taxation. Why income taxation leaves a positive sign is difficult to tell. Since it is the lag of income taxes that matters, it may be more than pure short-term endogeneity created by economic growth. There are good arguments for the case that tax-financed public goods may enhance growth and employment (Garrett, 1998; Boix, 1998), but, as mentioned before, our results do not allow us the possibility to indulge in the question of whether public spending is actually productive. For the purpose of the argument followed here, it is safe to say that income taxation seems to be less harmful than other taxes. In Germany, finally, taxation shapes labour market outcomes, though the effect is predominantly derived from payroll taxation. If the level of taxation of the previous period increases by 1 per cent, private sector employment drops by nearly the same amount. Germany is also an example of countries that have shifted the tax mix from income and payroll to indirect taxation with few labour market benefits.

The control variables in Table 3.1 show that labour market reactions differ between the three countries. The test statistics show that autocorrelation and – at least for the German case – nonstationarity still distort the results, a fact that is in line with findings of labour economists (Franz, 1993: 363). A theoretical explanation of the empirical distortions is the high correlation between the overall tax burden and indirect taxes. Supplementary time-series analysis (not shown) suggests that the overall tax burden is positively associated with employment only in the Swedish case – but it is weaker than for the three different forms of taxation. Hence, although there is some danger of confusing the impact of tax mixes with the impact of overall excessive tax burdens, this danger should not be overstated.

All in all, the results have important consequences for the subsequent discussion. First, country-specific effects are crucial in understanding the link between taxation and employment. Taxation alone cannot resolve this problem, even though tax forms differ in their impact on national labour markets. Second, country-specific effects foster the suspicion that labour market regimes differ between these three countries, and that these differences might explain whether taxation matters or not. As expected by Daveri and Tabellini (2000), tax effects are presumably smaller in the 'atomistic' and flexible US labour market and higher in continental and northern European countries. This is, of course, no direct proof for the impact of labour market institutions on the tax employment link, but it does foster the case for this.

Consecutive cross-sections

We have seen that the tax-employment relationship differs over countries, but does it also differ over time? For this purpose we assume that all countries behave similarly and analyse the cross-temporal evolution for the pooled sample. Table 3.2 shows consecutive cross-section regressions for 18 OECD countries over six points in time beginning in 1971 and ending in 1996. I begin with a look at control variables. Differences in unemployment are significant in the explanation of private sector employment. This epitomizes the severe employment problems of some countries. It is also important to understand why the usually positive long-term co-evolution

Table 3.2   Cross-section results for six periods

	Business sector employment to working-age population					
	1971	1976	1981	1986	1991	1996
Intercept	63.11***	35.38**	56.75***	51.25***	56.04***	50.27***
	(10.12)	(15.31)	(10.99)	(9.45)	(8.49)	(10.73)
Unemployment	−3.10***	−2.03***	−1.62**	−1.31***	−1.42***	−0.82**
	(0.55)	(0.54)	(0.32)	(0.27)	(0.27)	(0.28)
Wage	0.29	0.69*	0.36	0.49***	0.46***	−0.54**
	(0.24)	(0.34)	(0.21)	(0.15)	(0.14)	(0.19)
Income taxes	−0.51	−0.53	−0.53*	−0.47**	−0.21	−0.26
	(0.32)	(0.32)	(0.25)	(0.21)	(0.20)	(0.21)
Payroll taxes	−0.99***	−0.66*	−0.64**	−0.73***	−0.72***	−0.61***
	(0.27)	(0.31)	(0.21)	(0.14)	(0.17)	(0.18)
Indirect taxes	−0.09	0.16	−0.04	−0.09	−0.57	−0.67**
	(0.26)	(0.34)	(0.30)	(0.21)	(0.28)	(0.32)
Adj. R^2	0.75	0.23	0.77	0.91	0.93	0.89
Nobs.	18	18	18	18	18	18
F-Test	10.04**	3.88**	7.38***	22.48***	30.19***	18.73***

Note: Levels of significance: * < 0.10, ** < 0.05, *** < 0.01

of wage and employment is only visible for some years. In 1996 higher wages even seemed to reduce employment rather than increase with it. Income taxation is not of significant importance for employment levels. As far as the other two sources of taxation are concerned, a temporal pattern seems to be suggestive: throughout most of the period investigated, payroll taxes exert a negative impact on private employment; in the 1990s, indirect taxes also show a negative impact on employment for the first time.

Nevertheless, the evidence is not sufficient for corroborating the hypothesis that there are strong cross-temporal differences. One reason is the limited robustness of the results. Finland and Japan are important outliers because the model underestimates their employment performance. In addition, Australia and New Zealand are significantly below the average of the model. Additional variables do little to improve the situation. Wage inequality as measured by the OECD (1996), for instance, does not help greatly in accounting for these outliers. It is interesting to note that antipodean welfare states perform worse than the average, although both Australia and New Zealand rely on income taxation as the most important source of funding for their welfare states. Clearly, this deviation cannot be explained by tax mixes. New Zealand and Australia share high levels of targeting (Korpi and Palme, 1998) as well as a comparatively low degree of progressiveness in income taxation. In New Zealand, in particular, personal income tax does not exempt low-wage workers (Ganghof, 2006: 9). This could mean that the implications of income taxes for labour markets in these countries are more akin to those of payroll taxes in other countries (see Messere, 1993).

Several cross-sectional tests have been performed to control for the overall tax burden. This could explain the deviant position of Japan – which is the country with the lowest overall tax burden in the sample – but not that of other outliers. Finally, regressions with relative tax shares, i.e. individual tax forms as a percentage of total taxation, reveal equal or even stronger results for payroll and indirect taxes. It seems plausible, therefore, to assume that the tax mix matters – even once controlled for the overall tax burden.

All things considered, the regressions show a role for the tax mix. It is obvious that econometric problems and sample selection loom large in the findings. Country effects are plainly visible once time-series are compared. This finding is reasonable given the discussion of different theoretical models of labour markets. Taxes matter differently in different labour markets, and their influence over the persistence of unemployment is also different. Hence, I have to be very cautious when I proceed to the presentation of results for pooled data.

Pooled Estimates for Employment and Unemployment

Pooling data on aggregate (un-)employment

I use a data set of 17 OECD countries for the period between 1971 and 2001. Two transformations of the data have been performed: annual observations have been replaced by five-year averages; differences in the new observations have been computed in order to account for the problem of non-stationarity. The set of control variables includes GDP growth and gross wages, that is total compensation of employees relative to GDP. The two variables catch effects of variations in output and the wage sum. This should mitigate the problem of reverse causality induced by measurement problems in tax revenues.[16] Since unemployment poses both theoretical and empirical problems of collinearity, it has been dropped as an independent variable. Instead, unemployment features as a new dependent variable in separate regressions in order to account explicitly for cross-national differences.

Table 3.3 shows econometric results for private sector employment as a proportion of the working-age population and the unemployment rate. Whereas in the case for employment both fixed time- and country-effects were necessary, the equation with unemployment as the dependent only includes fixed time-effects. Multicollinearity does exist in both equations, but only to a limited degree. First-differencing did indeed eliminate autocorrelation. Cross-sectional correlation, finally, could not be rejected according to the test statistics. Since heteroscedasticity also haunts all models reported so far, I use panel-corrected standard errors instead of the simple ones (Beck and Katz, 1996).

The signs of the tax coefficients follow the expected pattern. Payroll and indirect taxes reduce private sector employment and increase unemployment. A change of 1 per cent in indirect taxation, in particular, decreases employment by 0.5 per cent and raises unemployment by another 0.5 per cent. No significant negative impact of income taxation can be derived from these results. According to Table 3.3, growth and wages are only relevant for private sector employment. Unemployment, in turn, is not affected by either of the two. This is in line with research conducted by labour economists, who have investigated the sluggish behaviour of unemployment in relation to growth and it shows clear signs of market imperfection (Bean, 1994).

An exception to the general rule is Ireland, an important outlier in both regressions due to its strong labour market recovery in later periods. Nevertheless, Ireland does not contradict the argument proposed here. Although Ireland has a high proportion of indirect taxation, the tax-mix has been shifting towards income taxes in recent decades. In general,

Table 3.3   Pooled results for employment and unemployment

	Business Sector Employment (First Difference)	Unemployment (First Difference)
Intercept	−2.986***	2.673 ***
	(0.917)	(0.576)
GDP growth	0.700***	−0.231
	(0.165)	(0.178)
Wage	0.025***	−0.044
	(0.007)	(0.054)
Income taxes	−0.069	0.076
	(0.152)	(0.127)
Payroll taxes	−0.511*	0.470**
	(0.313)	(0.266)
Indirect taxes	−0.574***	0.534***
	(0.202)	(0.221)
Adj. R^2	0.48	0.31
Nobs.	85	85
Fixed Effects	Time, Country	Time
F-Test (no FE)	2.87***	4.35***
Condition Index	8.79	12.699
AR(1), N(0,1)	1.32	0.37

Notes:
Levels of significance: * < 0.1, ** < 0.05, *** < 0.01.
Observations are first differences of five-year averages; 17 countries, five periods.
Coefficients of Fixed Effects (FE) not shown.
Panel-corrected standard errors in parentheses.
Condition index for multicollinearity.
AR(1), N(0,1): asymptotic test for serial correlation in residuals.

sensitivity analyses show that the three tax forms maintain significance even if influential cases such as Ireland are excluded. It is important to stress that the two equations presented here measure first-round effects only. Little is said about indirect effects via lower GDP growth or changes in the capital–labour ratio.[17] All things considered, the idea that payroll and indirect taxes matter more than income taxes is justified on the grounds of these models. Income taxes exert only a moderate influence on both employment and unemployment. Payroll and indirect taxes matter much more drastically for labour market performance at least in the short-term perspective.

Pooling sectoral data
The last question of interest in this section is to show whether there are sectoral differences for the impact of taxes on employment. A question of

Table 3.4   Pooled results for sectoral data

	Business Sector Employment Level	
	Employment in ISIC3 (First Difference)	Employment in ISIC6 (First Difference)
Intercept	−2.002***	−0.070
	(0.775)	(0.255)
GDP growth	0.559**	0.239***
	(0.261)	(0.088)
Wage	0.311	0.468**
	(0.264)	(0.246)
Income taxes	−0.061	−0.018
	(0.117)	(0.053)
Payroll taxes	0.260	−0.145***
	(0.179)	(0.059)
Indirect taxes	0.124	−0.127
	(0.325)	(0.143)
Adj. R^2	0.64	0.45
Nobs.	56	56
FE	Time	none
F-Test	(no FE)	2.407*
Condition index	10.34	6.82
AR(1), N(0,1)	1.49	0.82

Notes:
Levels of significance: * < 0.1, ** < 0.05, *** < 0.01.
14 countries, four periods (five-year averages).

major interest posed in the previous section dealt with differences between highly productive sectors and those with low levels of productivity producing (non-tradable) goods and services. I start with the two sectors manufacturing (ISIC3) and trade, restaurants and hotels (ISIC6). Again, the underlying assumption is that productivity levels are considerably higher in ISIC3. As in the previous case, the data have been transformed from annual observations to first differences in five-year averaged data. The exogenous variables are the same with the exception of wages which are now industry-specific and operationalized as total compensation of (private sector) employees in the sector relative to GDP.

Table 3.4 shows the result of pooled regressions for both ISIC3 and ISIC6. Whereas fixed time effects were necessary in the case of manufacturing employment, the equation with service sector employment as the dependent does not include any fixed effects. The table shows that employment in both sectors is driven by growth, whereas wages only matter for ISIC6. This could imply that a strategy of competitiveness and high productivity resulted in a form of insulation of ISIC3 against genuine labour costs. As has been suggested above, this finding would also make it clear that employment in manufacturing is – ex post – not very sensitive to taxation. Not one of the three tax forms seems to harm this sector. This pattern does not hold for ISIC6 which not only responds positively to wage increases in a typical long-term manner, but also negatively to increases in payroll taxation.

As expected, payroll taxation seems to be particularly problematic for low-wage sectors. Since the regression on ISIC3 includes fixed country effects, it is tempting to test whether the effects are statistically similar within welfare state clusters. As a matter of fact, Wald's statistics reject most of the attempts to cluster welfare states. One exception is Scandinavia, but with only three countries – Sweden, Norway and Denmark – this fact does not support a strong case for assuming regime-specific effects. Several other empirical tests have been performed to evaluate the robustness of the estimations. I used both the total tax ratio and OECD indicators of the effective tax burden. In both cases the effects were much larger for ISIC6. However, results for ISIC6 do not hold for all non-tradable sectors. If I ISIC6 replace by ISIC9, for instance, the sign of the tax coefficient changes, but maintains its significance. ISIC9 consists of social and personal services such as health or education services. It is therefore plausible to assume that tax variables such as payroll taxes are directly related to these kinds of public expenditures (Kemmerling, 2003).

To conclude, the results moderately corroborate the hypothesis that the problem of taxation differs across economic sectors. Non-tradable sectors that largely coincide with sectors of low pay seem to suffer more from labour taxes, namely in the form of high social security contributions. Note that the causality remains unclear, since such effects may be due to either differentials in productivity or international competitiveness, or both.[18] But the finding itself is fairly robust and leads to some (preliminary) conclusions. It is hence time to summarize the main findings of this chapter.

CONCLUSIONS

The main findings of the theoretical overview show that policy recommendations depend on the labour market approach chosen (see Table 3.5). In the table T stands for income, S for payroll and Z for indirect taxes. The assumptions are that the tax base of indirect taxation $Z(x)$ is bigger than that of income $T(x)$ and of payroll $S(x)$, that tax progression is highest for income taxes $T'(x)$, followed by payroll $S'(x)$, and indirect $Z'(x)$ taxes,

Table 3.5   A synopsis of theoretic results

	Tax Base	Progression	Insurance
	$Z(x) > T(x) >$ $S(x)$	$T'(x) > S'(x) >$ $Z'(x)$	$S \sim B > T \sim B >$ $Z \sim B$
CM	$Z \geqslant T \geqslant S$	$Z \geqslant S \geqslant T$	$S \geqslant T \geqslant Z$
WBT	$T \geqslant Z \geqslant S$	$T \geqslant S \geqslant Z$	?
EWT	?	$Z \geqslant S \geqslant T$	$S \geqslant T \geqslant Z$

Note: Rank ordering symbol $\geqslant$ shows tax form with best labour market outcome.
Inequality symbol $>$ shows tax form with a bigger base, a higher progressivity or more insurance.

and that the insurance component, symbolized by the relationship to benefits B, is highest for payroll taxes, followed by income and indirect taxes. The table shows a stylized rank ordering of the three tax forms in terms of employment effects. For example, the competitive model (CM) holds that the tax base of indirect taxes (Z) is best for employment, followed by income (T) and payroll (S) taxes. In general, the CM seems to endorse indirect taxation, whereas the wage-bargaining model puts income taxes in the most favourable light. Efficiency models produce results that are most difficult to summarize and lead to no clear winner.

Taken together, three points merit repetition. First, in a second-best world progressivity is not a bad thing. The reason is that it decreases wage pressure, especially if one assumes a wage-bargaining model. One must be careful with its normative implications, since the employment effects are positive only under specific theoretical and empirical assumptions, but these are not unrealistic. Next, in a second-best world a broad base may not always be a good thing. Only in the case of the competitive model it is clear that general consumption taxes should be less harmful. Exempting sensitive sectors such as the low-skilled could theoretically improve labour market performance in wage-bargaining and efficiency-wage models. Third, even from an insurance perspective contribution-financing is not necessarily preferable for the low-wage sector. Insurance via redistribution is a more viable option for poor people.

The empirical section has tested the relationship of tax forms on employment outcomes. There is evidence that payroll and indirect taxation have much more visible and detrimental effects on taxation than those of income taxation. The cross-country results are not 'infallible', but relatively robust. This pattern depends on country differences much more than on temporal evolutions. And most importantly, this pattern is more obvious in the so-called low-wage sector, as illustrated by ISIC6. On basis of this evidence, switching the tax base from payroll to income taxation may not be a bad idea after all. Ultimately, such a policy recommendation hinges on the question how to account for the political endogeneity of taxation. If there is some evidence that countries as diverse as Sweden and the US have a more employment-friendly tax mix (Scharpf, 2000; Kemmerling, 2005), so why is this tax mix on retreat over time (see Chapter 2) and why do some countries shift more and more income taxes to payroll and indirect taxation? For these questions we need political theory.

NOTES

1. This chapter builds upon surveys on the impact of taxation on labour markets (Bean, 1994; Layard *et al.*, 1991; Goerke, 2002).
2. They would, for example, allow for an impact if workers are close to the minimum wage. Looking back to nineteenth-century Germany, Bismarck might not have been wrong after all, since most workers then were extremely close to the standard of living required for reproduction.
3. The following discussions are necessarily highly selective. For more in-depth analyses see Blundell and MaCurdy (1999).
4. 'We know that the absolute value of the constant-output elasticity of demand for homogeneous labour for a typical firm, and for the aggregate economy in the long run, is above 0 and below 1. Its value is probably bracketed by the interval 0.15, 0.75, with 0.3 being a good 'best guess'.' (Hamermesh, 1993: 135)
5. Note that the second option of shifting forward the burden on to consumers is only possible with an 'accommodating' monetary policy (for example Homburg, 2003: 129) and opens the floor for a whole new set of intervening factors determining the interplay between taxation and inflation.
6. The OECD was particularly interested in the question of legal incidence between employers' and employees' social security contributions. Given the assumptions about demand being more elastic than supply, this approach has been called the 'Invariance of Incidence Proposition' stating that it does not matter who pays payroll taxation.
7. In these cases, consumption tends to be highly elastic, and producers are simply driven out of the market. The paradigmatic case is the increase in self-service (Kemmerling, 2003).
8. This is also true for another first-best tax which is lump-sum taxation. It does not play an important role in any OECD country.
9. The ratio of corporate to personal income tax revenues is typically one to four in OECD countries (Ganghof, 2000: 625). De facto, the incidence analysis of corporate income taxation shows that some 75 per cent of this tax is rolled over (Disney, 2000; Homburg, 2003).
10. The fact that Nickell and Layard (1999: 3058) report a negative impact of progressive income taxation on productivity in the long run seems to corroborate such a view.
11. They could point to countries like New Zealand which applied this policy reform. The so-called 'Rogernomics' reforms of the 1980s cut the top marginal income tax rate from 66 to 33 per cent in 1988, while social benefits were downsized simultaneously. Arguably, New Zealand's improved employment record since then has been a consequence of these reforms.
12. Manow (2002), for instance, has called the dominant mode of clustering into Scandinavia, Anglo-Saxon countries, and Continental Europe 'The good, the bad and the ugly'.
13. ISIC stands for the International Standardization of Industrial Commodities. Here I use Rev. 2 with overall ten major categories.

14. For a detailed descriptive analysis see Kemmerling (2003).
15. For all three regressions we run a model without the tax variables and compared it to the model which includes them. The F-test shows whether there is a systematic difference between the two.
16. As stated in Chapter 2, aggregate tax ratios to be analysed with caution (OECD, 1999b: 28). In particular, since tax revenues are expressed as proportions of GDP, they are prone to problems of reverse causality. A decrease (increase) in employment leads to a decrease (increase) in revenues and will automatically induce a 'perverse' sign for regressions with employment or unemployment as the dependent variable.
17. In an accompanying paper (Kemmerling, 2005), I also dealt with the problem of cross-temporal instability of the tax coefficients. The hunch was that this problem probably arises due to deepening international economic integration. The results were in line with this claim.
18. For a discussion of the role of international economic integration see Wood (1994) or Blanchard and Wolfers (1999).

APPENDIX

To show that taxation has a negative impact on employment with some level of redistribution, I follow a model of labour supply as depicted in Laisney *et al.* (1995). Individuals maximize consumption (*C*) and leisure time ($L = 1 - N$) given a standard utility function

$$max[U(C_i, L_i)] \qquad (3.6)$$

s.t.

$$I + [w_i(1 - \tau)N_i - C_i] + \varphi[B_1 w_i(1 - N_i) - C_i]$$
$$+ (1 - \varphi)[B_0(1 - N_i) - C_i] \leq 0 \qquad (3.7)$$

Equation 3.7 is a budget constraint that consists of exogenous income *I*, income from labour and two kinds of social benefits. The first type is indexed on the net wage $w_i(1 - \tau)$ with a replacement rate of B_1. N_i corresponds to the number of working hours on the individual level or the number of employed people on the aggregate level (see pp. 33–34 on this). The second type is a flat rate transfer B_0. Both are weighed with factors (φ, $1 - \varphi$) that add up to one. φ can be seen as the relative share of redistributive to proportional transfers in a social security system. The first order conditions (FOC) are

$$\frac{\partial U}{\partial C} = \lambda \qquad (3.8)$$

$$\frac{\partial U}{\partial C} \geq \lambda[w_i(1 - \tau) - \varphi B_1 w_i(1 - \tau) - (1 - \varphi)B_0] \qquad (3.9)$$

as well as the budget Equation 3.7. Equation 3.9 shows that the amount of leisure chosen depends on the tax rate τ as well as the benefit levels B_0 and B_1. This equation delivers a criterion for the individual to join the labour market or not (to simplify we set $I = 0$).

$$[w_i(1 - \tau)N_i - C_i] \geq \varphi[B_1 w_i(1 - \tau)(1 - N_i) - C_i]$$
$$+ (1 - \varphi)[B_0(1 - N_i) - C_i] \qquad (3.10)$$

which, after transformation gives

$$\frac{N_i}{1 - N_i} \geq \varphi B_1 + (1 - \varphi)B_0/[w_i(1 - \tau)] \qquad (3.11)$$

The last equation shows that the level of employment depends on taxation for $B_0 > 0$. Thus, in social security systems with a minimum amount of redistribution, there is a relationship between taxes and employment additional to the mere substitution effect. Let the RHS of Equation 3.11 be denoted reservation wage R, as the opportunity costs of working. Following a simplified version of Nickell and Layard (1999: 3048), the union wants to maximize the utility of its members and firms, given w_i, choose N_i, the labour demand to maximize profits π_i. This yields the Nash product

$$N_i[w_i(1 - \tau) - R]^\beta \pi_i \qquad (3.12)$$

with β as the bargaining power of the union *vis-à-vis* the employers. The FOC with respect to w amounts to

$$\frac{w_i(1 - \tau)}{w_i(1 - \tau) - R} = \frac{\beta\eta s_\pi + (1 - s_\pi)}{s_\pi} \qquad (3.13)$$

where η is the wage elasticity of demand for labour and s_Π is the share of profits in value added. If we assume a balanced government budget, we have the following public budget constraint

$$tw_iN_i = \varphi B_1 w_i(1 - N_i) + (1 - \varphi)B_0(1 - N_i) \qquad (3.14)$$

If we solve for B_0 and assume that w is either the median or the mean wage of union members – depending on the specific form of Equation 3.1 – we get

$$B_0 = \frac{wtn - \varphi B_1 w}{1 - \varphi} \qquad (3.15)$$

with $n = N/(1 - N)$. Plugging the last equation into Equation 3.13 and solving the latter for n yields

$$n = \left[\frac{s_\pi}{\beta\eta s_\pi + (1 - s_\pi)} + \varphi B_1\right]\left(\frac{1 - \tau}{\tau}\right) \qquad (3.16)$$

This equation shows that for rising tax rates, the ratio of employed to non-employed people decreases and the inverse holds for unemployment. The tax effect is larger for higher levels of redistribution in a welfare state as measured by φ.

4. Political economy applied to tax mixes

In Chapter 2 we saw that the relative importance of income taxes from country to country, and that there is also a switch away from income taxes in most countries. In Chapter 3 I argued that this trend against progressivity was not to the benefit of employment. There is evidence that the switch away from income taxation hurt employees with low wages more than others. If policy-makers are pure social planners, they should have reversed this trend. The question arises when governments have the capacity to reform their tax systems and why they want to do this. The prime task of this chapter lies in delineating the political motives for labour taxation in more detail by paying attention to the key political conflicts and the institutional rules that govern these conflicts.

The chapter is organized as follows: I will start with a general conceptualization of the research question within the framework of political economy. I will use the standard concepts of political economy: preferences, restrictions, institutions. In the second section, these distinctions will guide a survey of the literature on the determinants of the tax mix. I will relate different claims to each other and gauge their theoretical consistency and empirical validity. In the third section I will develop an argument that complements and refines some of the previous findings. In particular I will defend the position that while the overall intuition about the politics of progressivity is correct, i.e. left parties favour it more than right parties, institutionalized insider–outsider cleavages in the labour market weaken the labour alliance for income taxation. These intra-class conflicts are part of the reason why it proved to be relatively difficult in recent years to halt the erosion of progressivity in the tax mix.

POLITICAL COMPETITION AND THE TAX MIX

There is a rapidly expanding body of literature dealing with political economy approaches to the political system which is too vast to be summarized here. For the more specific question on tax mixes, the chapter will deal with the most common notions and compare their results where necessary.[1]

For political economists the first fundamental question is the dimensionality of a policy issue, since multiple dimensions make distinct political equilibriums less likely and the political decision inherently more difficult (Hinich and Munger, 1997; Roemer, 2001). It is important to note that the dimensionality of the policy space is not the same as the dimensionality of the voter space. As long as the policy issue at stake is one-dimensional, political equilibria may be tractable although voters differ in several dimensions (Roemer, 2001: 26).[2]

Dimensionality

To get an idea about the dimensionality of the tax mix I will make some stylized assumptions about each tax form and compare them. Roemer (1999) says that in a world with wages as the only source of income a typical income tax problem is two-dimensional. To this insight I add the specific (though simplified) functional forms that relate taxation to wages for payroll and consumption taxes:

$$\tau_{inc} = \tau_1 \times w^2 + \tau_2 \times w + \tau_3$$

$$\tau_{pay} = \begin{cases} \tau_1 \times w & \text{for } w \leq \overline{w} \\ 0 & \text{for } w > \overline{w} \end{cases}$$

$$\tau_{con} = \tau_1 \times c \times w \tag{4.1}$$

The three formulas show that the dimensionality of the tax form varies. For a simple functional form of a progressive tax such as (personal) income taxation three parameters τ_1, τ_2, τ_3 have to be determined. τ_3 is a simple version of a basic income threshold and typically has a negative sign, that is income taxes are paid beyond the threshold.[3] τ_1 and τ_2 are parameters that make the income tax progressive, that is increasing with wages w. For a given tax burden one parameter can be expressed with the help of the other two, so the dimensionality of this (simplified) income tax system is two (Roemer, 1999). In the case of a proportional payroll taxation τ_{pay} with a ceiling for contributions there are two parameters. One parameter accounts for contributions to be subtracted from gross wages, and another for the wage ceiling imposed $(\overline{w})$. Hence the system is at least one-dimensional for a given tax burden. Finally, a typical consumption tax has only one parameter. In this case, the political conflicts over the total tax burden and over indirect taxation conflate if the system consists only of indirect taxes.

Though these distinctions do not reflect the full diversity of tax problems, they already reveal some important information. For instance, simplifying a bit, one may say that indirect taxation is not a real political issue in itself for given levels of total taxation. Theoretically it is no coincidence that both Beramendi and Rueda (2007) and Kato (2003) that left governments with preferences for higher spending will eventually also prefer higher levels of indirect taxation, for given levels of income and payroll taxation. Another implication of these differences is that political competition changes its nature with the number of tax parameters involved. Broad and simple tax forms such as VAT tend to follow the logic of general redistribution, whereas complex tax schedules invite interest groups lobbying for loopholes and package deals will ensue (Hettich and Winer, 1999).

One Dimension

The most famous example of a one-dimensional tax model is Meltzer and Richard (1991). The authors assume one (proportional) tax form, a flat-rate benefit to all, and an elastic labour supply. There are only two competing parties, and voters' preferences are defined in such a way that a political equilibrium exists. The voters differ only in one dimension, namely between poor and rich relative to average income. Voters have the following utility

$$U_i(c_i, x_i) = W_i(\tau) \tag{4.2}$$

Direct utility U_i depends on individual consumption c_i and individual leisure x_i, both of which depend on the tax rate τ. Therefore, one also knows the indirect utility W_i of voter i which depends on the tax rate. Voters face a budget constraint BC_i:

$$BC_i \leq c_i - (1 - \tau)wl_i - B \tag{4.3}$$

The voter can only consume as much as he works l_i times the net wage $(w(1 - \tau))$ and what he receives from the government B. After solving the indirect utility of a voter for τ every voter has an ideal tax rate (for example Persson and Tabellini, 2002: 120), and since voters only differ in their income or productivity all poor voters prefer higher taxes and all rich voters prefer lower taxes. In this case preferences and the policy space are such that one can apply the traditional median-voter theory. Hence the politically chosen tax rate is the tax rate of the median voter and depends on two variables: the degree of income inequality measured as the distance between median e^m and mean income e, and the elasticity of labour supply with respect to taxation L_τ (Persson and Tabellini, 2002: 121):

$$\tau^m = \frac{e^m - e}{L_\tau(\tau^m)} \qquad (4.4)$$

The equation shows that the politically chosen tax rate, the tax rate preferred by the median voter τ^m, rises with income inequality and decreases with higher elasticity of labour supply. Both the voter and the policy space are one-dimensional. This is due to the fact that the level of flat rate benefits B can be expressed as a function of tax rates τ and mean income e. Politicians can therefore decide upon one of the two tools, and this automatically determines the other.

Multiple Dimensions

A switch from income to payroll or indirect taxation implies multidimensionality. Hettich and Winer (1999) develop a model to explain tax structure. They assume that an incumbent government faces one opposition party and that this government optimizes a set of tax policies to gain political support. To make their results comparable with our interest in the tax mix I will assume that governments have only three policy instruments: $\tau_h \varepsilon \{\tau_{inc}, \tau_{pay}, \tau_{ind}\}$, as well as a flat-rate social benefit B. As in the Meltzer-Richard model there are $1 \ldots i$ voters who derive utility from consumption c_i and leisure x_i. Voters utility U_i is indirectly affected by three policy instruments (W_i), since taxes determine how much voters want to work and consume.

$$U_i(c_i, x_i) = W_i(\tau_{inc}, \tau_{pay}, \tau_{ind}) \qquad (4.5)$$

A highly stylized budget restriction for an individual (BC_i) would be the following

$$BC_i \le c_i - \{(1 - \tau_{ind})[(1 - \tau_{inc} - \tau_{pay})wl_i + (1 - \tau_{inc})s_i + B]\} \qquad (4.6)$$

The individual budget restraint of Equation 4.6 depends on three forms of income: the amount of individual labour supply (l_i), the amount of savings (s_i), and a lump-sum government transfer (B), which is also the reservation wage. All three forms are subject to indirect taxation, whereas income from savings yields income taxes, and labour income yields income and payroll taxes. Voters will choose their work–leisure combinations on the basis of this tax mix, but voters will also differ in their preferred tax mix. Since we now have three policy instruments given a certain level of B, Hettich and Winer use a probabilistic voting model in which governments have an expectation of how voters respond to changes in tax policies, that is they are not certain about them. Governments maximize the support S which I formulate in a simplified way:

$$S = \sum_i \sum_h f_h^u u_i \tag{4.7}$$

for all three tax forms ($\tau_h \varepsilon \{\tau_{inc}, \tau_{pay}, \tau_{ind}\}$) and all voters ($1 \ldots i$).

This equation says that the support for the government party is a weighted sum of taxpayers' utility. This sum consists of the responsiveness of each (class of) voter to changes in any of the three tax forms (f_h^u) and the utility of the taxpayer thereby derived (u_i). According to Hettich and Winer's 'representation theorem' (ibid.: 69), the complete form of the model looks like this:

$$\Lambda = S + \tilde{\lambda}[BC_{gov}] + \sum_i \sum_h \lambda_{ih} L_{i\tau_h} \tag{4.8}$$

for all voters $I = 1 \ldots i$ and all three tax forms.[4] In our case the government budget constraint amounts to

$$BC_{gov} = \tau_{ind} c + (\tau_{inc} + \tau_{pay}) l + \tau_{inc}(1 - c) - B \tag{4.9}$$

and l, c, s are the average labour supply, consumption and savings.

The representation theorem says that policy makers have to optimize Equation 4.8, that is they have to maximize a weighted sum S of individual political reactions towards tax changes (first term) subject to the public budget constraint BC_{gov} (second term) and the constraints imposed by the individual elasticities of labour supply (third term) to each tax form. The latter are denoted by L_i with respect to $\tau_h \varepsilon \{\tau_{inc}, \tau_{pay}, \tau_{ind}\}$. This formulation is equivalent to a Nash solution between two political parties where both parties are uncertain about voters' preferences and both opt for the same political platform. If all voters are equally represented, and there is no special interest group with higher political clout, no bias exists and the political competition model leads to a Pareto efficient outcome with several tax rates. This basic result does not change even if voters are allowed to react once the tax system is set up. Individuals may have an incentive to change their behaviour so that they fall under a different form of taxation, for instance they could give up work to avoid payroll taxes altogether. This does not change the tax structure.

To derive concrete results, one would need to impose more structure on the model (Kemmerling, 2006). It is obvious that the model is still simplistic, since it does consider the different functional forms of taxation as exhibited in Equation 4.1. Nevertheless a look at the equations already exhibits some interesting messages. Most importantly, given the model structure it is quite likely that income and payroll taxes are political substitutes, whereas for realistic elasticities of the tax base, indirect taxes are political complements with the other two forms. Intuitively, the reason is that people shift between saving and consumption, working and not working, so that a government will use tax forms on all of these activities. The theory hence corroborates our earlier findings on the correlations between different tax forms (see Chapter 2).

We see that the importance of one tax form depends on in how far people can evade this form of taxation relative to others by working less (L_{it_h}). I will call this effect an explanation of the tax mix based on 'restrictions'. A government will also use a tax form less, if this tax form reduces individual utilities (f_h^u). I will call this an explanation based on 'preferences'. The Hettich and Winer model is very simplistic in its assumptions about the political process, which corresponds to a probabilistic voting model between many voters and a government. However, differences in the set of political institutions may also lead to differences in the tax mix. I will call these institutional explanations. In the following section I will briefly turn to each of these three major types of explanation.

REVIEW OF THE LITERATURE

All in all, the Hettich and Winer model is still very much stylized, but it gives us an idea how a politico-economic model for a switch from income taxation will look like. In particular it will contain three different types of determinants: preferences deduced by some data on voter heterogeneity, restrictions or costs of policies induced by processes such as internationalization of markets and institutions as rules of distributing power and aggregating preferences. Using these distinctions I can now compare competing claims of the scholarly literature on the determinants of the tax mix.

Preferences

Whereas individual hetereogeneity is largely treated as a nuisance in economics, it is the very essence of politics if one thinks of politics as the art of finding collective decisions for solving divisive issues. Unsurprisingly, many accounts of variations in the tax structure are based on differences in the electorate and, in particular, on (partisan) ideology. Most prominently, scholars have related partisan ideologies to the overall size of taxation and spending (for example Schmidt, 1982). Accordingly, the 'left' should favour higher spending, whereas the (secular) 'right' should favour lower taxation. This logic can be extended to the tax mix and the issue of progressivity. It is obvious that progressive income taxation has been on the leftist agenda from the very beginning (Marx, 1989 [1848]). As Figure 1.2 has shown partisan argument is not easily visible in the case of the tax mix. Traditionally liberal or conservative countries such as the US or the UK have similar or higher proportions of income taxes than Sweden.

As a line of defence, Beramendi and Rueda (2007) argue that left labour parties had to shift preferences to overall spending, given that internationalization made income taxation increasingly different. This implies that left parties still have the same underlying preferences, but they needed to adjust policy preferences because of external restrictions. Ganghof (2006) shows that – after controlling for institutional and international factors – the traditional left-right cleavage is an important part in the explanation for or against progressive income taxation. Nevertheless, countries like Sweden have shown that social democratic welfare states still make heavy use of income taxation. Similarly Boix (1998) and Garrett (1998) find an influence of social democratic strategies in the configuration and importance of capital taxation.

Related to partisan-based explanations are those that focus on the positions of the rich versus the poor. As argued in the previous section on the Meltzer-Richard model, poor people can tap into rich people's wealth by increasing taxation. In the context of the tax mix, this should imply that poor people prefer progressive income taxation to other tax forms. This assumption is generally acknowledged, but it is difficult to prove the demand for progressive income taxation in a Downsian framework (Hindriks, 2001). Using more sophisticated models, Roemer (2001) finds a stable poor versus rich outcome after controlling for other cleavages (see also Gould and Baker, 2002). The cross-country record of empirical findings is mixed, since reliable indicators are hard to construct (Milanovic, 2000; Lindert, 2004). Given that the demand for or against income taxation may also depend on tax base effects, it is natural to ask whether some people do not simply vote those taxes down that affect them the most. For instance, pensioners enjoy preferential treatment in direct taxation and therefore may fear indirect taxes most.

Alternatively, one may think that voters demand insurance rather than redistribution. If people differ in their exposure or willingness to take risks, this could shape their demand for insurance-based tax forms. Compared with inequality and wealth there is no dominant indicator how attitudes towards risks are distributed in the electorate. One way is to conceive of any member of a society as risk averse, but let exposure vary across groups. One could think that those groups that are more likely to be unemployed are also those who demand more insurance (Rehm, 2005). In a similar way,

Iversen and Cusack (2000) assume that the extent of deindustrialization is a good proxy for the amount of risk aversion in a society.[5] An alternative indicator of risk exposure is asset specificity, defined as the transaction costs that are involved in transforming (geographically or functionally) one specific asset into another (Williamson, 1988). One such asset is human capital (Estevez-Abe *et al.*, 2001), since some jobs require high, but specific levels of qualification. People investing their time and money to acquire these skills cannot freely move to another occupation without losses in income. The more specific their assets, the higher their demand for insurance (Iversen and Cusack, 2000; Iversen and Soskice, 2001). Unfortunately, all these indicators have little to say about other sources of risk aversion, or about the preferences of the non-working population.

How do these alternative claims fare in a stylized cross-country perspective? As a brief check we will use the following hypotheses: higher relative wage inequality (Franzese, 2002) should result in more income taxes and less payroll and indirect taxation due to the redistributive character of tax progression. High levels of deindustrialization should mirror preferences for payroll or income taxes. I will assume that the dependent (elderly) population dislikes indirect taxes and favours payroll or income taxes.[6] These claims are subjected to a somewhat naive first empirical test. The dependent variables are the three ratios of one tax relative to the other two. For example, $t1rel$ is income taxes over the sum of payroll and indirect taxes. We see that our hypotheses are confirmed for wage inequality. Higher values show lower levels of inequality. The table shows that for a large difference between average and median wages the share of income taxes decreases and payroll and indirect taxes increase. More ambivalent is deindustrialization (Iversen and Cusack, 2000), as our measure of insurance seekers. As expected the share of income taxes is higher, but the shares of payroll and indirect taxes are lower. The lack of evidence may be due to the problematic character of this indicator. Finally the share of old people decreases, as expected, the share of indirect taxes and increases the share of payroll taxes. It does decrease, however, the share of income taxes. It goes without saying that these numbers are pairwise correlations and do not allow for a strong causal interpretation.

Explanations based on cleavage theories have several shortcomings. First, other cleavages unrelated to the policy area may simply dominate the policy formation process. According to Wagschal (2001) religion continues to play an important role in explaining the differences of tax systems across countries. Kersbergen (1995) argues that Catholic socialism was the driving force of continental European payroll taxation with lasting effects. Some political economists argue that religion or racism simply supersede the economic cleavages in a population (Roemer, 2001: Chapter

Table 4.1   Correlation of different measures for the voter space

	t1rel	t23rel	t5rel	(A)	(B)	(C)
Relative wage	−0.242	0.232	0.308	1.000		
inequality (A)						
	0.000	0.000	0.000			
	646	646	646	966		
Deindustrialization	0.229	−0.105	−0.290	−0.089	1.000	
(B)						
	0.000	0.003	0.000	0.017		
	785	785	785	713	887	
Proportion of	−0.289	0.335	−0.236	−0.017	0.388	1.000
elderly (C)						
	0.000	0.000	0.000	0.634	0.000	
Nobs.	786	786	786	752	860	913

10). In these cases retrospective economic voting, that is punishing politicians who make tax choices against voters' interests, is not very strong (Kitschelt, 1994). Given these problems of operationalization and salience of preference-based explanations, a different school of thought has focused on the role of restrictions in the politics of taxation.

Restrictions

From the model of Hettich and Winer we know that the tax structure will follow the rule of inverse elasticities. The higher the responsiveness of a tax base, the higher its political costs and therefore the lower its level of taxation. This prompts the question what determines this responsiveness. Clearly one answer is geographic mobility, as numerous contributions have shown (Wilson, 1999; Brueckner, 2003), but it is not the only one.

There is a rapidly growing literature on the role of tax competition in the determination of tax levels and structure. As in the case of cleavages a theoretical foundation lies in the concept of asset specificity. Among others Boix (2003) argues that many forms of capital are much more fungible and less specific than labour and that this leads to a downward pressure of capital taxation. Given that international integration has been on the rise in recent decades and barriers to capital mobility have been dismantled, this tendency should have increased (for example Genschel, 2002). International integration therefore tips the balance towards indirect taxes as the least mobile, whereas income taxes on unspecific assets that are easily transferable should be lowest. Payroll taxes should rest somewhere in between given that labour mobility tends to be lower than capital mobility, but the relocation of firms should ultimately also have an impact on the taxability of labour income. Among others Swank and Steinmo (2002) find that internationalization and competition on capital taxation also drag taxes on labour income down. The existence of unemployment can enhance tax competition since it leads governments to lobby for international capital on a higher than optimal level (Huang quoted in Wilson, 1999: 271).

We should not expect these effects to be large in the short run. Some very open economies such as Denmark or Sweden manage to maintain high levels of income taxes without conclusive indications so far that they will follow a long-term downward trend (Ganghof, 2006). Neither is there clear evidence for cross-national convergence on rates or ratios (see Chapter 2).[7] The consensus of the literature is that there is some conditional convergence between sufficiently similar countries. One key tenet is that countries have to be differentiated between smaller and larger ones, since only the small ones reap a strategic benefit in engaging with tax competition (Kanbur and Keen, 2001; Wilson, 1999). Though the empirical basis of this claim seems fairly sound for the case of (corporate) income taxation (Ganghof, 2006), we do not quite know why this is the case. The US tax cut of 1986 triggered a series of tax cuts in other countries and shows that gains and losses of capital can be substantial even for large countries (Dehejia and Genschel, 1998). Moreover, country size is a wildcard character for many different factors. Borck (2002), for instance, argues that large countries also have higher levels of voter heterogeneity, perhaps leading to higher political immobility. In a similar way it has been argued that veto players or domestic politics inhibit competition (Hallerberg and Basinger, 1998; Basinger and Hallerberg, 2004).

In political terms voters' responsiveness to taxation has many other origins. Hettich and Winer mention the costs of tax administration and surveillance. Technical innovations will play a role here, since many contemporaneous tax forms such as VAT would have not been possible without modern techniques of tax administration and levy. Responsiveness may also be a function of absolute size and visibility of the tax burden. Taken together this implies that new tax forms follow a certain life cycle. Indeed, growth rates of comparatively new taxes such as VAT have been highest for all major tax forms in recent years (see Chapter 2), but the momentum of growth rates has already declined. One reason lies in the fact, that VAT itself induces evasive action, for instance if economic activity submerges into the shadow market (for example Schneider, 2002).

Political costs of taxation may also include subjective reasons. Many scholars have argued that people do not have the required information to discern all forms of taxation equally, and some taxes are supposed to be less visible than others (OECD, 1995: 10). Of course, the crux is in which taxes these are. Some authors believe indirect taxes to be less explicit, since people do not see them on their payrolls (for example Kato, 2003). However, one could argue that it is the employers' part of the payroll taxes that is the most elusive. In this sense workers only reckon with their own tax payments and the standard Invariance of Incidence Proposition does not hold (Sanandaji and Wallace, 2003). Finally, since even tax experts have problems to understand the income tax code in many countries, fiscal illusion could also play a role for income taxation. And yet a well informed union, for example, should factor in all these taxes when it comes to bargaining. All in all, the visibility argument does not procure much guidance, unless we know more about the taxpayers' responses to tax policies.[8]

A last class of factors influencing responsiveness effectively 'switches off' politics, that is they generate automatic adjustments. Messere (1993) shows that the income taxation rises with inflation and growth, since both variables shift more people into higher income brackets. A larger dependent population will automatically lead to higher levels of social security contributions. Unfortunately, these factors are hardly exogenous to the political process itself, since politicians have to agree on these forms of automatic drift. Moreover, for these questions it is important to consider the role of political institutions. The latter have a strong impact on the frequency of political changes, and maybe also on the direction of change if they systematically favour certain groups of voters over others.

Institutions

A third strand of approaches deals with the impact of political institutions on the tax mix. There are two different versions of this strand: First, institutions may shape the tax mix and bias it towards one of the three tax forms. Public choice theorists, for example, think that institutions affect the strategic incentives of actors and therefore alter the tax mix directly (Mueller, 2003; Persson and Tabellini, 2003). Second, institutions affect the speed of adjustment towards a new outcome which is ultimately due to changes in preferences or restrictions. In this respect institutions are veto points or institutional constraints that hamper the speed of political adjustment (for example Immergut, 1992). Here I will deliberately focus on directional effects of major political institutions, since only the directional effects are specific to the question of the tax mix, whereas the latter are a question of the general responsiveness of politics.

An important distinction in political institutions is between majoritarian and proportional voting systems (Lijphart, 1994; Persson and Tabellini, 2003). The scholarly literature has agreed on a roughly stable though not flawless empirical observation: proportional systems produce higher public budgets and more taxation than majoritarian ones (Persson and Tabellini, 2003).[9] For the case of the tax mix, the picture is more diverse. Some authors (Hays, 2003) say that proportional systems favour minority preferences and thus lower the burden on (corporate) income taxes. Others (for example Rhodes, 2000), however, argue that majoritarian systems shift the tax system from progressive to regressive tax forms. Cusack and Beramendi (2006), finally, argue that it is a combination of executive and electoral institutions that shapes the mixture of labour and capital taxation.

As for the executive dimension, the literature has argued for a different impact of presidential versus parliamentary systems on the growth of government (Lijphart, 1994; Mueller, 2003). Parliamentary systems also seem to generate broader social transfer programmes and its concomitant systems of funding, whereas presidential systems tend to pit minorities against each other, thereby increasing the relative weight of specifically targeted expenditures (Hettich and Winer, 1999: Chapter 11). Given the bargaining between presidents and parliaments, an income tax system serves special provisions in the income tax code best. Historical analysis has corroborated this finding for the case of the US (Steinmo, 1993).

There is not much comparative literature on the direct influence of independent (supreme) courts and judicial review on the tax mix. Some authors even doubt whether courts act as effective veto players, since partisan actors tend to be more radical than judges and absorb the courts' positions (Tsebelis, 2002). Ganghof (2006), however, finds that the German supreme court played a vital role in the reforms of income taxation by effectively filtering out more radical proposals. Judges also defend individuals' entitlements and thus maintain or even enhance the system of social security contributions. Other than that it is difficult to make general theoretical claims given the level of aggregation of tax mixes.

Federalist institutions provide a more promising institutional forum for the politics of the tax mix, although preference formation of lower-tier governments are sometimes difficult to derive. This is the case when representatives' partisan and regional interests diverge. Recall the historical case of nineteenth-century Germany, where the 'Länder' refused to introduce a tax-financed insurance system because of the fear that it would concentrate revenues at the central level. Instead, they created a para-fiscal authority with its own political agency which was, by and large, independent from both Länder and Reich governments. A more recent example is the German tax reform of 2000. The social-democratic government managed to push

Table 4.2   Mean comparisons of taxes and political institutions

	t1rel	t23rel	t5rel	ttgdp
Majoritarian versus proportional voting system				
No	0.649	0.405	0.616	33.586
Yes	1.189	0.280	0.476	31.942
Presidential versus parliamentary system				
No	0.894	0.349	0.504	35.566
Yes	0.776	0.465	0.431	32.751
Judicial Review				
No	0.963	0.357	0.432	35.849
Yes	0.807	0.386	0.522	34.342
Federalist institutions				
No	0.732	0.392	0.610	33.847
Yes	0.880	0.344	0.5159	29.783

through the reform against a conservative majority in the second chamber, by 'bribing' federal states in which Social- and Christian Democrats were in coalition governments (Zohlnhöfer, 2001). In the US, Hettich and Winer (1999) argue, federal and state-level tax policies are largely independent, whereas in parliamentary federalist systems such as Canada or Germany they depend on each other which explains not only differences in the level but also the funding of welfare spending. Mueller (2003: 226) surveying the literature on this topic, concludes that fiscal federalism can also result in redistribution not from rich to poor regions, but in the form of pork-barrelling.

Given the lack of conclusive theoretical findings of political institutions on the evolution of the tax mix it is tempting to probe some of the available data. Table 4.2 gives a stylized empirical record for four different institutions comparing group means of countries to which the institution either applies or not. The tax variables are defined as before in Table 4.1, apart from *ttgdp* which is total taxation relative to GDP. It has to be stressed that the distribution of institutions across countries is non-random and that within countries autocorrelation is high. Therefore the empirics of Table 4.2 are not enough to gauge the validity of the causal claims surveyed in this section. It is nevertheless interesting to see whether these data confirm the claims made in the literature. A look at the table shows that except for the distinction between majoritarian and proportional electoral systems there are few strong findings for the tax mix. Majoritarian systems seem to generate relatively important income taxes. The level of the tax burden, measured as the tax-to-GDP ratio *ttgdp*, is, as expected, slightly higher in proportional systems.

MAIN ARGUMENT

Introduction

Surveying the literature has yielded some important determinants that shape the tax mix. International competition may explain some of the uniform trends over time against progressive income taxation. Political institutions catch some of the cross-country diversity which is inherently stable across time. Preference-based explanations seem somewhat weaker. Inequality may play a role over time, but it is clearly not exogenous and across country a well-known reverse relationship holds.

Nevertheless, relatively robust restrictions-based explanations beg the question why defence mechanisms against the relative decline of income taxes failed in some countries, but not in others. This prompts an investigation of key actors in defence of income tax. So let us round up the 'usual suspects': the political left. One way to explain the decline of tax progression is that the left has become weaker over time in many countries. Corneo (2005) and Alt *et al.* (2007) made this argument for the German and UK case respectively. Traditional left parties are under strain in most party systems (Kitschelt, 1994), their core electorate is on decline for various political and economic reasons. And yet, rising global inequality should actually strengthen the left agenda. I argue that there must be something in addition to external constraints that hampers the link between left power and tax progression. This is the existence of internal conflicts between workers of different kinds. The issue of tax progression has certain side effects that drive fissures through the interest coalition of labour and weakens its cause. In a nutshell, tax progression weakens the efforts of wage compression and enhance competition at the bottom end of the wage scale. Tax progression also affects the bargaining power of trade unions. We will deal with each of these claims in turn.

Tax Progression and Job Rationing

No matter how accountable democratic institutions are many policies lead to incongruence between those who govern and those who are governed. Tax policies are no exception to this, as the example of more or less encompassing tax bases showed (see Chapter 2). The incongruence is very obvious in the realm of labour market regulation in which institutions affect people with different skills and job prospects differently. Employed workers will vote for the regulation of labour markets, given it makes jobs safer and possibly enhances wages. The same institutions make reentry for unemployed more difficult. This is the political cleavage between insiders and outsiders (Lindbeck and Snower, 1986; Saint-Paul, 2000). The cleavage hinges on the existence of rents for being employed relative to being unemployed. If there is such a rent, insiders have an incentive to defend it against outsiders.

Are these rents plausible? Theoretically, rents are to be expected if supply of a relatively abundant factor is restrained *vis-à-vis* a relatively fixed factor. In Saint-Paul (2000), for instance, highly skilled labour is a fixed factor, whereas unskilled labour is abundant. In this case, unskilled labour has an incentive to redistribute via the imposition of labour market regulation, that is imposing an artificial scarcity of labour. This generates a conflict between insider employees and the newly created, unskilled outsiders in the labour market. It is people with lowest skill levels who bear the brunt of unemployment, leaving the intermediate skill levels better off. In this view, the insider-outsider cleavage overrides the traditional cleavage between capital. 'Labour' as a coalition of all workers could only extract rents if capital supply is fixed, but this is not a reasonable assumption given technological changes and internationalization of markets (Saint-Paul, 2000).

Is there empirical evidence that labour market institutions generate rents? One may directly try to measure rents. Saint-Paul (2004) finds some, albeit weak, evidence on the aggregate level, whereas micro-data shows more significant indications of rents in certain (protected) occupations (Clark, 2003). A more indirect test is to analyse the economic consequences of institutions. As numerous surveys have shown, this is an equally difficult enterprise in which few clear results emerge (for example Layard *et al.*, 1991; Bean, 1994). Take employment protection for instance. The research on layoff protection has yielded ambivalent effects on employment and output (OECD, 1999a). Empirically it seems to decrease job turnover and increases long-term unemployment (OECD, 1999a). Another example is union strength, usually measured as higher union density. It may enhance insider power and exercise more leverage when bargaining for wages. Some studies (Nickell and Layard, 1999; Borjas, 2004) find a positive effect on unemployment, wages and wage compression, although these findings have not remained uncontested (Calmfors and Driffill, 1988; Checchi and Lucifora, 2002). As a third example economic theory has argued that unemployment benefits reduce the search effectiveness of the unemployed. This, in turn, decreases the competition between unemployed and employed and enhances the insider power of the latter. Again, the empirical record of this proposition is mixed (Nickell and Layard, 1999: 3053). And yet, in all these examples it is clear that regulation does not benefit all workers equally, and quite possibly harms workers with lower skills.

Let us assume that there is a cleavage between insiders and outsiders in the labour market. How does this cleavage between skilled and unskilled people affect the choice of tax system? If institutions truly generate rents, those protected by these institutions have an incentive to vote for them (Saint-Paul, 2000). The unemployed people should rather back liberal policies (Saint-Paul, 2000: 37). Therefore rent-generating institutions are only likely as political outcome if pivotal voters face less risk to become unemployed. In this case rents are concentrated among the employed. Saint-Paul focuses on a narrow conception of labour market institutions, and follows the traditional literature in arguing that taxation has no impact on unemployment via wage bargaining. As shown above, however, if taxation and expenditures are not the same, taxation will have an effect on employment. It will become a form of labour market regulation (see Chapter 3). This implies that political complementarities between redistributive taxation and labour market institutions are likely to exist. With lower taxation, rich (highly skilled) people are better off. With some level of job protection, intermediately skilled workers are better of. Proportional taxation therefore unites middle and upper class against the unemployed (Saint-Paul, 2000: 79).

This argument is necessarily simplified, but can be extended in several ways. First, according to Pierson (1996) welfare state policies are frequently path dependent. Reform, he says, is particularly difficult to achieve where institutions create their own political constituency. Insidership gives a formal account of such bias towards the status quo, because voters want to protect their rents. This bias is enhanced if there is uncertainty about outcomes of reforms, since voters can no longer identify themselves either as winners or losers from a political (Saint-Paul, 2000: 222). Second, the key insight does not depend on a median voter model. Austen-Smith (2000) and Lee and Roemer (2005) use more complex models of the political process to argue that higher tax rates kick low-wage workers out of the labour market, increase wages and also increase the consumption of the average worker. Finally, the results may change if one adds an insurance motive to the existence of taxation and regulation. In Moene and Wallerstein's (2001) and Iversen and Soskice's (2001) analyses voters will vote for institutions to guarantee some level of contingency claims. Unless this reverts the redistributive character of regulation, it leaves the main message for the tax mix unchanged.

It is crucial to remember that for some models of unemployment at least (see Chapter 3), progressive taxation limits the rent-extracting capacities of the employed relative to the unemployed. In this case progressive forms of taxation become less attractive for the employed in labour markets where insider power is strong. Labour market institutions therefore indirectly decrease the likelihood for progressive income taxation relative to payroll or indirect taxation. Payroll taxation, in turn, may be a more effective means of discouraging workers in the low-wage sector than minimum wages or other forms of taxation. To put it more bluntly, labour votes for higher taxation of its own tax base if intra-class conflicts occur. They will favour payroll taxation or indirect taxation to income taxation, since the former do not exempt low-wage workers from paying taxes. Income taxes do exempt these workers and thereby reduce much of the crowding-out effect in which the median voter is interested.

This is a very strong version of a claim that is historically not very plausible. Do institutions come into existence because of rents? Arguably not. Saint-Paul shows that in a competitive labour market all workers dislike institutional regulation, since their welfare is lower with than without regulation. This tells us something about the time when most of social and labour market policies were created. At that time labour markets were arguably more competitive. In the late nineteenth century, unemployment insurance emerged after serious crises in early manufacturing (Agell, 2002). The Roosevelt administration's New Deal was an immediate response to the Great Depression. Many historians would agree that demand for insurance was a key 'driver' of welfare statism (Lindert, 2004).

Hence, some refinements of the initial argument are necessary. As long as taxation was about the construction of a welfare state, and labour markets did not generate any institutionalized rents, taxation was predominantly about taxing capital. The existence of mature welfare states and possibly the opening up of international markets have changed this. Taxation is nowadays more and more about taxing labour and as such conflicts within labour are likely. In addition, job rationing induced by labour taxation does not need to be a zero-sum game. If taxing the low skilled leads to positive shocks in productivity, and is accompanied by efforts to increase workers' skills, it will be to the benefit also of lesser skilled workers. If productivity effects merely lead to rationalization or markets are in recession, taxation will hit lesser skilled people even more (Blundell and MaCurdy, 1999).

Of course, tax policy is not first and foremost about labour market regulation. But it has important side effects for labour markets that drive wedges into the interest coalition of workers. Tax mix decisions are hence not unlike other examples of policies in which (left) labour politics acts seemingly against itself. For the realm of active labour market policies and employment protection Rueda (2005) finds similar effects both on the micro and macro level. In particular, he finds that labour market protection is more strongly favoured by those with good job prospects than outsiders of the labour market. If this is true we would expect a relationship between employment protection, and hence insidership, with tax progressivity.

Taxing the working poor

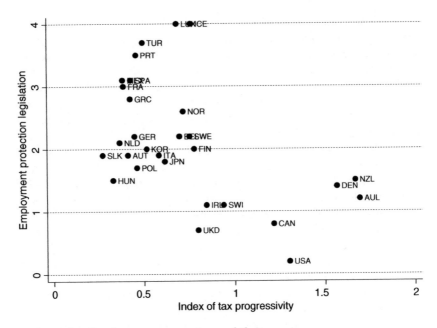

Figure 4.1   Employment protection and the tax mix

Figure 4.1 shows that for the connection between the strength of employment protection legislation (see Chapter 5) and the relative importance of
income taxation for the year 2000. The relationship is clearly not perfect,
but a downward-sloping curve is clearly visible. As expected countries
with high levels of employment protection are those in which payroll and
indirect taxes dominate the tax mix.

Let me give a final, anecdotal example for a case when left political
actors opted for higher taxation of low-paid jobs. This happened in the
case of minor jobs in Germany. These jobs, so-called '620DM'-jobs,
earned an income up to 310 Euros a month and were until 1998 exempted
from income and payroll taxation. Some 13 per cent of the employed were
registered owners of such a minor contract (Wagner, 1998). With the new
coalition government between social democrats and greens in 1998, the
regulation of these jobs was modified so that a lump-sum for social security
contributions had to be deducted from 1999 on. This reduced the number
of these jobs in 1999 by around one million and slowed the growth of these
jobs thereafter (Rudolph, 2003). Although the official aim of this reform
was to stabilize revenues for social security, these minor jobs posed real
threats to those workers with similar jobs but fulltime contracts. That was
the key reason why unions and the Social Democrats were against these

jobs. The example shows that there is a cleavage between fulltime workers and holders of minor jobs. The reform of the tax system clearly was to the benefit of the former and to the damage of the latter. It also shows that left parties were torn between two core values: 'decently paid work' and 'full employment'. The clash in the rhetoric of the left mirrors the underlying conflicts of interest.

Wage Bargaining and Tax Progression

Hettich and Winer (1999) allow for different political weights of voters, but they do not deal with the specific variations in political influence. In their empirical calibration, they find that capital taxation fell less than expected in the US between 1973 and 1983 and ascribe this to a rise in the political power of poor voters (ibid.: 186). Aside from the fact that the US saw a major tax cut not long after 1983, this finding is not very satisfying, since we still want to know who are the pivotal players and how they manage to influence the tax mix. One way is to assume the existence of powerful lobby groups (Olson, 1965) that bargain with politicians for tax reductions. This makes sense in the case of corporate taxation, since producer groups vary in many different aspects such as sunk costs (Alt *et al.*, 1999). Since we are more interested in broad forms of taxation, whose incidence ultimately falls on labour, enterprise-driven lobbying is arguably less important. A further intricacy is that exceptions and special provisions in personal income taxes or payroll taxes are frequently found to be given to groups that are not explicitly organized. Ganghof (2006: 40), for instance, mentions the preferential treatment of house-owners and pensioners.

As the discussion in Chapter 3 showed, the organization of industrial relations has important effects on wages and employment. Neither unions nor employers' associations are restricted to bargaining on wages. They also have a political role in that they lobby governments. Two examples may show the active engagement of unions in the political process of tax reform: Schwartz (2000) argues that Australian trade unions put up a substantial fight against the introduction of general sales taxes, whereas a 'new labour' government in New Zealand was able to push a similar bill through without serious resistance. A priori it is hence likely that unions do have an interest in taxation, but it is unclear in what direction this interest goes.

Political scientists have traditionally modelled the relationship of unions and governments along the lines of the neo-corporatist hypothesis of exchange (Meidner and Hedborg, 1984). The idea is that in countries where the interests of governments coincide with those of trade unions – due to the hegemony of social democratic parties – trade unions exert wage moderation but are compensated by increases in the social wage and hence taxation. This argument has been applied and modified in various ways (for example Scharpf, 1987; Garrett, 1998) to explain cross-country divergence in macroeconomic performance. Along the years it has become more and more obvious that crucial results depend on the preferences and restrictions of unions as well as the strategic interactions with employers and the state.

As in the literature on the economic effects of wage bargaining, the fundamental question is what unions actually want. Wages for unions members is surely very important, but maybe it is also wage compression or unemployment (Oswald, 1982). Iversen (1999), for instance, suggests that trade unions care not only about wages and unemployment, but also about wage equality. Under such circumstances trade unions back proposals to enhance the social wage as a means of achieving wage compression. The crux, however, is that this holds not only if unions are sincerely preferring wage compression but also if they want to enhance their own wage bargaining power by keeping low-skilled employees out of the market. Different assumptions about unions' preferences clearly breed positive and negative views about unions neither of which could be easily refuted (Checchi and Lucifora, 2002).

Given these controversial normative stances, many authors have rather looked at the restrictions union face as well as their institutional embeddedness. In a seminal article, Calmfors and Driffill (1988) use Olson's logic of external effects to suggest that the level of bargaining shapes unions' preferences in two ways: first, the more centralized the system the less product market competition will be dominant at the firm level. Second, the more centralized the system, the larger the special interest group becomes and hence the more likely it is that this group will internalize negative effects such as inflationary pressure. This makes unions on intermediate levels fighting most aggressively for wage increases and thereby augmenting unemployment.

Their argument has evoked a litany of theoretical and empirical rejections and modifications. Clearly, other institutional features of the wage bargaining system such as union concentration or the level of coordination have an influence on trade unions' behaviour (Kittel, 2001, 2003). In the realm of wage coordination, there are many functional equivalents to centralized coordination (for example Traxler *et al.*, 2001; Kittel, 2001). Moreover, many factors influence the empirical relationship between wage bargaining institutions and macroeconomic output. Trade union behaviour may, for instance, be very different in small internationally open economies (OECD, 1997a). The outcome is also dependent on the product market regime and the organization of the business sector (Soskice, 1990). Further, the theoretical results become very difficult to predict if institutions and union membership are thought to be endogenous. A final critique is that the social wage is a public good, so it is not clear whether trade unions really benefit from its provision (Iversen, 2000: 209). Mares (2006), for instance, argues that the welfare state is increasingly for labour market outsiders so that the effectiveness of wage restraint has severely decreased. A long-term rise in unemployment is the consequence.

In this book the burden shifting between insiders and outsiders is part of the explanandum rather than the explanans. All the aforementioned studies show that the (institutionalized) configuration of trade unions has a clear impact on their strategic incentives. A commonality of many of these attempts is to gauge the 'representativeness' of trade unions: in how far is their congruence between those workers that have influence on a (tax) policy and those who are affected by it. Union density is typically taken as the prime indicator for monitoring this congruence, with larger unions being more representative for total labour force. However, labour market regimes differ in many aspects. Most prominently, bargaining coverage has a strong impact on representativeness, since high coverage means that even if union density is low, the outcomes of the bargaining process can still affect large factions of the workforce. Take, for example, the case of France where union density hovers slightly above 10 per cent, but wage bargaining affects nearly 90 per cent of all workers.

Bargaining coverage is defined as the relative proportion of people affected by collective bargaining of industrial partners. Since not all employees have equal rights in terms of collective bargaining, adjusted rates include only those workers who could, but do not have to, be affected by these wage negotiations (Traxler *et al.*, 2001). Common practices between unions and employers or mechanisms of legal extension lead to the fact that coverage rates are usually higher than rates for union membership. Since these extension mechanisms differ from country to country, coverage rates are also very different. Ochel (2001) has collected information on adjusted coverage rates from various sources. Whenever possible, I have updated the country series with the help of various sources.[10] I have shown elsewhere that this indicator, far from being perfect, reveals some of the political importance of trade unions (Hartlapp and Kemmerling, 2008). The relationship between union density and bargaining coverage is related to the tax mix as Figure 1.2 of the introduction shows. Moreover, in most countries bargaining coverage and union density increasingly diverge: whereas coverage has become more extensive, with some notable exceptions, union density has been on decline in most countries except those with a Ghent system.

How can we understand this negative relationship between tax progressivity and (excessive) bargaining coverage? I argue that trade unions with a limited degree of representativeness are no natural allies to progressive income taxation. There are two reasons for this: one based on the idea of decent jobs and the crowding out of the low-skilled sector, one based on the influence of tax progression on wage bargaining. I have already dealt with the former reason so I can be brief here. Unions with a limited degree of representativeness will arguably over-represent workers with medium skill levels. Workers with higher skills fear high tax progression, since they are directly affected. Workers with low skills are usually the first to drop out of unions (Riley, 1997; Schnabel, 2003). The remaining unionized work force, will lobby for policies in their interest, and tax progression rather increases than hinders competition on the low end of the wage scale.

The second reason needs more elaboration. Let's make an extreme example: tax-based wage policies. In times of high economic turbulence, that is high inflation and high unemployment, it has been suggested to use a high prohibitive level of taxation to curb inflation (Wallich and Weintraub, 1971). It remains a controversial issue whether this means is effective at all, but it has been applied several times. For instance, several Eastern European countries applied such measures in the aftermath of economic transition during the 1990s. It is no coincidence that unions did not like tax-based income policies at all (Greskovits, 1998), since they seriously hamper any bargaining potential against employers. Whenever used, tax-based income policies are a short-lived phenomenon dealing only with extreme situations of inflation.

Nevertheless, tax-based income policies may have more general implications. These policies are designed to tax wage increases at prohibitively high levels. This is an extreme version of tax progression. In normal times high tax progression in the medium range of wage income taxes more of wage increases away from unions. *Ceteris paribus* it decreases the effectiveness of wage bargaining and reduces average wage increases and, for rather general conditions, increases employment (see Chapter 3). If trade unions are not very encompassing, but have some market power, they prefer tax systems with proportional taxes since these leave their own bargaining position unaffected. They prefer these taxes to progressive ones, since the latter could undermine their *Tarifautonomie*, that is their autonomy to bargain over wages with employers without state intervention. If trade unions are very large and encompassing, they are automatically limited in their bargaining scope (Calmfors and Driffill, 1988). In these cases they do not really care about the tax structure itself, but about the level of total taxation (Iversen, 1999).

The debate on corporatism and macroeconomic policies has provoked three major critiques: the neglected role of employers, the government, and the central bank. Is this critique also detrimental for a proposed relationship between the representativeness of unions and the progressivity of the tax mix? In the strategic setting of wage bargaining employers may have an indirect effect, if they make unions change their behaviour. Remember that only in the standard monopolistic wage-bargaining model with atomistic employers trade unions set wages unilaterally so as to maximize their preferences. However, the difference in tax effects between a unilateral model of union monopoly and a bilateral model of unions and employers' associations is not strong (Goerke, 2002). Employers' associations themselves have similar incentives to crowd out low-wage competition in a national economy (Haucap *et al.*, 1999). Like unions, employers' associations are beset with conflicts between members with higher and lower productivity, so it is very likely that fewer productive firms are under-represented. Under such circumstances employers' associations do not change the impact of unions' final policy preferences on the tax structure.

The strategic role of the government matters if governments do not merely act on behalf of left voters or unions. In general, lobbying makes sense if governments have objectives somewhat different from the pivotal voter, as interest groups can change political preferences to their liking. As an example Palokangas (2003) constructs a model for bargaining between employers, unions and governments. He assumes that employers and unions lobby the government on capital and labour taxation and labour market regulation. If it is easier to tax wages rather than income from profits, governments will do two things: they will first tax labour more heavily than capital – this mirrors the standard argument of tax theory, since elasticities are higher for capital; and second they will introduce labour market regulation which enhances the wage-bargaining power of unions. The reason for the second effect is that higher bargaining power translates into a higher wage share in the economy and this will automatically increase tax revenues for the government. Employers are better off since they do not pay capital taxation, whereas unions get some leverage on wages so that all actors agree on a package deal combining labour market regulation and labour taxation. Since unions share this interest, the outcome should be similar to the one previously found: unions and employers have a disincentive to shift towards progressive income taxation. Governments respect this, if their key interest is the maximization of revenues.

CONCLUSIONS

Politico-economic approaches are very narrow in their assumptions about human behaviour. Rationalist approaches have been frequently criticized in the realm of tax policy making (for example Cox, 2001; Steinmo, 1993;

Swank and Steinmo, 2002). For instance, left politicians do have sincere concerns about 'indecent' jobs. This will affect their behaviour and makes them cautious against attempts to 'subsidize' low-wage work. However, we do not know whether politicians use these words sincerely or for strategic purposes. In addition, it is very difficult to show the strength and causal nature of such normative concerns (Kemmerling, 2007). More troublesome, the question about the tax mix yields different normative values into battle against each other. Should left parties endorse 'full employment' or the promotion of 'decent jobs'? If there is a trade-off between the two norms, political economy is all the more necessary.

Here is a brief recap of the argument so far: We have seen that in politico-economic models three different factors are important to explain the tax mix: preferences, restrictions and institutions. In the scholarly literature there is evidence for the causal impact of all of these. In particular, majoritarian institutions and tax competition seem to have a sizeable impact on the tax mix. Also, as the first two chapters have shown history looms large into the determination of the tax mix. Finally, short-term processes of economic adjustment do shape the tax mix.

As for preferences the evidence is weaker. Neither partisan nor poor-versus-rich models play a very visible role in the shaping of the tax mix. I think this is due to the fact that strategic environments of key actors depend on the underlying structure of the labour market. Left mobilization, in particular, seems to play a double role: On the one hand, it is certainly true that one needs to have strong left parties, preferably in interaction with strong trade unions, to achieve redistributive policies such as tax progressivity. On the other hand, unions themselves become ambivalent about their political pressure for higher progressivity, if they: (a) operate in regulated labour markets in which insider interests dominate; and (b) have much stronger political powers than economic relevance. Under such circumstances, we should expect unions and left parties to switch their behaviour and become less interested in tax progressivity. With these hypotheses in mind I now proceed to the empirical evidence.

NOTES

1. For an extensive survey of theoretical models of competition and the issue of the tax structure, Hettich and Winer (1999, Chapter 1) is arguably the best source.
2. Euclidean or spatial models, which are more popular in political science, tend to conflate the policy and voter space, but this yields consistent micro-funded results only in very special cases (Milyo, 2000). Simply put, the reason is that policy and voter preferences are not a bijective relationship, that is if one is aware of voters' preferences and restrictions, one also knows the policy preferences, but the reverse is not true.

3. There are other ways to reduce the tax burden for small incomes such as tax credits or zero zones.
4. All λ are La grange multipliers used to weigh the government decision problem.
5. In fact, many researchers (Iversen and Cusack, 2000; Kitschelt, 1994; Scharpf, 1987) have argued that deindustrialization has transformed the policy space, but it is rarely acknowledged that deindustrialization itself is endogenous to features of the welfare state (Kemmerling, 2003).
6 . I refer to Chapter 5 for details on these indicators.
7. Taxation on corporate income are an exception, since here the evidence for tax competition is strongest (Devereux *et al.*, 2002).
8. Taxpayers' compliance is also a difficult subject since it differs markedly across countries (Schmidt, 2000; Edlund and Aberg, 2002) and depend on perceptions and political preferences that are quite possibly endogenous (Lindbeck, 1995).
9. It is not flawless, since definitions of this distinctions differ and there many causal mechanisms for its explanation (Austen-Smith, 2000; Bawn, 1993; Franzese, 2002; Roemer, 2001).
10. For details see Chapter 5.

5. Empirical evaluation

In this chapter I will deliver some empirical tests for the relationship between left political preferences and the progressivity of the tax mix. The major claims were both cross sectional – why do some countries have a higher share of income taxation – and cross-temporal – why does income taxation decline in most countries. It is needless to say that such questions are difficult to pin down with any methodology in comparative political economy (Kittel and Winner, 2005). Instead, I follow the path of many contributions in the field that 'triangulate' several sources of empirical evidence (Iversen, 1999; Mares, 2006; Rueda, 2005). In particular, I will cross-validate quantitative findings for several countries with historical and case-study evidence. I use quantitative evidence to gauge the validity of my claims for a set of 20 OECD countries for some 30 years. In doing so, I have to restrict my analysis to coarse operationalizations of my key variables. The upside is that I can deal with some important issues such as competitive explanations. I use the historical analysis of nineteenth-century Germany to understand the importance of slowly changing variables such as the role of the welfare state. It also serves to remind us that historically the intuitive nexus between the left and tax progressivity is correct. Finally, I use a comparison of the UK and Germany after the Second World War to show that this nexus is not so clear any more. In the comparative case studies I can also do justice to the multidimensional characteristics of both the evolution of the political left and the evolution of tax progressivity.

QUANTITATIVE EVIDENCE

This section starts with a quick glance at empirical studies and the methodologies used therein. Next, I will discuss at some length the operationalization of my key independent variables. Finally, I will show some empirical relationships in levels. The next subsection shows pooled estimates for temporal changes and probes into the robustness of these findings. In particular, it deals with spatial dependence and endogeneity.

INTRODUCTION

State of the art

In the following I will stick to the dependent variable defined as the relative importance of income taxes relative to the other two major forms of labour taxation: payroll and consumption taxes. To the best of my knowledge, nobody has used this measure extensively before, but there are several related studies. Swank and Steinmo (2002) analyse the determinants of (Mendoza-type) effective tax rates on capital, labour and consumption taxes. They regress them separately on a battery of political, social and economic variables and use a pooled data set of 18 countries and 14 years. They use data in levels and a lagged dependent variable to control for serial correlation and fixed time and country effects. Their major results are that a measure for the liberalization of the capital account (Quinn, 1997) and structural unemployment reduce effective labour taxation, whereas Christian democratic parties and the lag of the unemployment rate enhance it.

Volkerink and Haan (1999) look at the economic and political determinants of taxation on personal income, social security contributions, and consumption taxes measured as tax-to-GDP ratios. They investigate over 20 countries over more than 30 years. They use a random-effects model in first differences. Their major result is 'that political and institutional variables do not substantially influence the actual shape of the tax structure' (p. 1). They split their sample temporally and find some effects of partisanship on tax spending for early periods.

Both Kato (2003) and Beramendi and Rueda (2007) analyse the determinants of consumption taxes. The latter authors show that the partisan effect changes signs across time. Simply put, whereas social democrats were once against taxing consumption, they nowadays use it increasingly as a source of public revenues. The authors estimate five year averages and include the lag of the dependent variable. Kato's major variable is an (instrumented) measure for social expenditure which she uses as a proxy for the increasing need for public revenue. Her measure actively engages with the problem of endogeneity, but the instruments chosen make her variable difficult to interpret.[1]

Cusack and Beramendi (2006) analyse effective labour taxes, including income and payroll taxes. Their key finding is that a high level of wage coordination together with left-wing governments enhance labour taxation. Their conclusion is that social democrats, once again because of higher overall demand for welfare spending, are forced to tax labour. Ganghof (2006) shows that lumping together taxes on corporate and personal income is problematic, since the determinants of both forms are different. He uses statutory rates and simple cross-section estimates to show that corporate taxation is led by internationalization and country size, whereas personal income taxation is primarily driven by income to total taxation.

International integration and its effect on tax competition has triggered a substantial amount of empirical research which is too vast to be summarized here. Many studies have found evidence for strategic competition of national tax rates in 'spatial' models (see below and Franzese and Hays, 2007; Swank, 2006; Winner, 2005). Hallerberg and Basinger (1998) find that the number of veto players slows the downward trend in corporate tax rates (but see Ganghof, 2006). Several studies have found that the internationalization and the liberalization of capital accounts shifts taxation from capital to labour (Schwarz, 2007; Adam and Kammas, 2007).

Operationalization of key independent variables

My most important indicators for labour market institutions are the level of employment protection legislation, union density and bargaining coverage of wage negotiations. Given the theoretical discussion I expect that employment protection and bargaining coverage represent sources of insider power and will therefore reduce tax progressivity, whereas union density represents the strength of left labour and will enhance progressivity. The difference between bargaining coverage and density I call surplus coverage and it shows discrepancies between the political and economic leverage of trade unions. It should be negatively related to tax progressivity.

As for the first, employment protection legislation, I use Blanchard and Wolfers' (1999) index. The authors combine and extend several measures that codify legal practices of employment protection and were developed by the OECD (1999a) and Lazear (1990). I updated this series with data from OECD (2004a). The summary measure ranges from almost no protection (0.2) in the case of the US to strongest protection (4.0) for Italy and Spain in 1970. Its temporal variation is much more limited and amounts to some 0.2 changes on average per decade. My second measure is (net) union density, that is economically active members of trade unions as a percentage of total labour force. I took the data from Ebbinghaus and Visser (2000) and updated it with new estimates for later years (Visser, 2006). Union density rates range from some 12 per cent in Spain and the US for 2004 to some 60 per cent in Sweden in the 1970s. In most countries density rates have fallen by as much as a third, but there are notable exceptions such as Belgium or Sweden. The third indicator is bargaining coverage, that is the legal practices to extend the results of wage negotiations of trade unions to other sectors of the economy. I used Ochel's (2001) indicator of bargaining coverage as percentage of those affected by wage bargaining relative to total labour force and updated it with information from several other sources.[2] The indicator ranges from nearly 100 per cent in Austria in 1970 to a mere 14 per cent in the US in 2004. Again, temporal variation is fairly limited: the average coverage dropped from some 75 per cent in the early 1970s to some 65 per cent in 2004. Data on union density and bargaining coverage can also be combined to an indicator of representativeness of trade unions (Hartlapp and Kemmerling, 2008). The simple subtraction bargaining coverage minus density shows whether unions have a higher leverage on wages and probably politics than their actual proportion in the labour force and the electorate.

All of these measures are necessarily crude and fraught with measurement problems in the international context. Moreover, they do not allow for a more fine-grained analysis of the structural composition of insiders. I will add this qualitative information later on. For quantitative purposes these aggregate indicators are the best I can think of, given the restrictions of availability and comparability of such data.

Cross-sections

In Table 5.1 regressions for four years (1970, 1980, 1990, 2000) are calculated in which the dependent variable is the relative importance of income as opposed to payroll and indirect taxation. Since there is only up to 20 observations I include very few independent variables: the three indicators of labour market institutions – union density, bargaining coverage and employment protection, the share of cabinet seats of social-democratic parties from Manfred G. Schmidt's data base,[3] and a dummy for the two antipodean countries. The latter is due to the fact, as shown in Chapter 2, that these countries have very different tax systems in which payroll taxes are virtually nonexistent.

Indeed the table shows that the inclusion of this antipodean dummy is necessary, whereas I do not find much evidence for partisan politics. As said before, both conservative and social-democratic welfare states have traditionally made use of income taxes, so this is not very surprising. Union density, however, is positively associated with higher proportions of income taxes. As expected, higher bargaining coverage is negatively associated with income taxes. Hence we see that there are offsetting tendencies in the representation of labour in politics. Higher membership fosters the case for more (progressive) taxation, higher coverage indicates the contrary. Employment protection legislation is only significantly related to the dependent variable in the latest year, but again the sign of the coefficient

Table 5.1   Cross-section results

	Income relative to payroll and consumption taxes			
	1970	1980	1990	2000
Intercept	1.21***	1.40***	1.20***	1.10***
	(0.26)	(0.14)	(0.14)	(0.14)
Union density	0.02**	0.01**	0.01**	0.01**
	(0.01)	(0.00)	(0.00)	(0.00)
Bargaining coverage	−0.14**	−0.15***	−0.01***	−0.00*
	(0.00)	(0.00)	(0.00)	(0.00)
Employment protection	−0.00	−0.03	−0.05	−0.22**
	(0.08)	(0.06)	(0.06)	(0.08)
Social democrats	0.00	0.00	−0.00	0.00
	(0.00)	(0.00)	(0.00)	(0.00)
Antipodeans	1.19***	1.75***	0.90***	0.87***
	(0.21)	(0.56)	(0.14)	(0.09)
R^2	0.84	0.81	0.81	0.82
Nobs.	17	20	20	20
F-Test	15.33***	15.58***	40.45***	50.87***

Notes:
Levels of significance: * < 0.10, ** < 0.05, *** < 0.01.
Robust standard errors in parentheses.

is as expected negative. Higher protection is related to fewer income taxes, not more. Given the high stability of the institutional variables over time, it is not surprising that the four regressions produce fairly similar results. Taken together they imply that the empirical evidence on the basis of cross-country variation shows the picture I expected.

Cross-sectional regressions with few observations are vulnerable to various sources of disturbance such as omitted variables. As evident in the survey of the empirical literature, few results seem to be really stable in different studies. The limited robustness of many of these findings prompts me to be very careful in choosing the right empirical strategy. As in the economics chapter I will now proceed to some pooled regressions between labour market institutions and my dependent variable. Institutions do not vary strongly over time, so it is by no means guaranteed that pooling will show similar results as in the analysis of cross-sections in levels. This is because I have to use temporal differences to get rid of problems of auto-correlation and stationarity. I will use fixed and random effects to look for commonalities in both types of regressions. Thereafter I will deal with two important econometric issues: spatial dependence and endogeneity.

Pooled Regressions

In a pooled model I can add more control variables to gauge the reliability of my results. For inflation I use the annual change in the consumer price index taken from the OECD statistic compendium. From the same source, I extracted information on the standardized rate of unemployment, the degree of openness (imports and exports divided by GDP) and growth in GDP. I use Armingeon *et al.*'s data compilation[4] for information on the proportion of elderly people in the total population. As an indictor of income inequality I chose Rob Franzese's measure (Franzese, 2002). It is based on manufacturing wages as a proxy for median income and GDP per capita as a proxy for average income. His measure ranges from 0.64 for Sweden to 1.80 for Greece.[5]

As for the political control variables I experimented with several measures of the strength of social democracy. As before, I use the share of cabinet seats of social democratic parties in government. Alternatively, I used data on median voter positions from Budge *et al.* (2001), in particular the measure of the left-right-position of the median voter as calculated by Kim and Fording (2001). Both variables are only available for legislative terms, so there is little annual variation. The temporal stability is even higher for constitutional variables. I use Persson and Tabellini's (2003) data base on political institutions in order to extract information on the distinction between majoritarian versus proportional voting systems.

The dependent variable shows a very high temporal stability over time, and in some countries it is even non-stationary. For this reason, I will only report results for first temporal differences. Having said this it is not surprising to find much less explanatory power of institutional variables in such a set-up. First differences remove most of the cross-country variation and focuses on much less pronounced differences in time. If anything, this methods works against the previous findings than to the benefit of them. Using first differences makes the inclusion of bargaining coverage difficult since it is the slowest changing variable. For this reason I combined the indicator of union density and bargaining coverage as described before. The new indicator describes the percentage of the labour force that is not member of unions, but nevertheless affected by their bargaining.

Pooled models

Table 5.2 shows the result for pooled regression with the dependent variable being the first differences of the relative proportion of income taxes. All independent variables enter in first differences with the exception of the dummy for antipodean countries, the dummy for majoritarian voting systems and GDP growth, since the latter already is a dynamic

Table 5.2   Pooled estimates

	Δ Income relative to payroll and consumption taxes			
	RE	FE	FE	FE
Δ_{t-1} Employment protection	−0.023	−0.018	−0.018	−0.018
	(0.017)	(0.020)	(0.021)	(0.020)
Δ_{t-1} Surplus coverage	−0.0020*	−0.0019*	−0.0019*	−0.0020*
	(0.0010)	(0.0011)	(0.0011)	(0.0011)
Δ Unemployment	0.000027	0.00061	0.0025	0.0029
	(0.0040)	(0.0048)	(0.0049)	(0.0049)
Δ Inflation	0.0071***	0.0060***	0.0061***	0.0061***
	(0.0014)	(0.0018)	(0.0018)	(0.0018)
Δ Openness	0.00042	−0.00057	−0.00045	−0.00045
	(0.00076)	(0.00099)	(0.00099)	(0.00099)
GDP growth	0.0065***	0.0069***	0.0067***	0.0067***
	(0.0017)	(0.0022)	(0.0022)	(0.0022)
Antipodean	−0.0089			
	(0.010)			
Δ_{t-1} inequality			0.29*	0.28*
			(0.17)	(0.17)
Δ old-age pop.			−0.0021	−0.0033
			(0.017)	(0.017)
Majoritarian system			0.029	0.029
			(0.056)	(0.056)
Δ social democrats			0.000013	0.000035
			(0.00015)	(0.00015)
Δ_{t-1} spatial lag				−0.34*
				(0.18)
Constant	−0.016***	0.034	0.031	0.039*
	(0.0060)	(0.022)	(0.023)	(0.023)
Observations	575	575	575	575
Number of countries	20	20	20	20
R^2	–	0.144	0.149	0.155

Notes:
Levels of significance: * < 0.10, ** < 0.05, *** < 0.01.
Robust standard errors in parentheses.

variable. The variables for labour market institutions enter as first differences of the previous year to avoid problems of short-term endogeneity. The four models differ in the number of regressors included and the specification used. The first two show the results for a random- and a fixed-effects model respectively. The fixed-effects model includes both time and country fixed effects, but suppresses their coefficients. Both models have well-known advantages and disadvantages for macro-aggregate data (Wooldridge, 2002). Fortunately, the results do not differ strongly between the two models. In particular the two major variables of interest, changes in employment protection legislation and representativeness have very similar coefficients in both models. Whereas there is no significant effect of short-term changes in employment protection on the tax mix, changes in surplus coverage work as expected: the larger the difference between coverage and membership becomes, the less important become income taxes. Levels of significance are not very high, but reasonable given the temporal stability of this variable.

The economic control variables are much stronger. Both growth and inflation lead to a higher proportion of income taxes. This reflects the well-known phenomenon of cold progression, that is more taxpayers automatically end up in higher tax brackets. It may also reflect the generally higher responsiveness of income taxes to economic booms (Messere, 1993). Changes in unemployment rates are unrelated to the dependent variable. The same goes for changes in the degree of openness, the only case in which even signs change going from the random to the fixed-effects model. The antipodean dummy does not play a role any more, since first differencing removes most of the cross-country variation.

In the last two columns of Table 5.2, I have extended the fixed-effects model by additional regressors. This serves as a check of robustness against omitted variables. Neither temporal changes in the seat share of social democrats in governments nor changes in the relative share of older people in total population affect the tax mix. There is also no difference visible for majoritarian systems. Only changes in income inequality do affect the tax mix in the third model. The theoretical prediction of this indicator is that higher inequality should lead to more (progressive) income taxes. Given the high probability of a reverse causality, redistributive taxes reduce income inequality, I have chosen to include only the first difference of the previous year. In this case the sign is as expected: Higher inequality leads to more income taxation.

Spatial dependence and international competition
The fourth model adds a final regressor to the previous model: a spatial lag. The introduction of a spatial lag serves two purposes: Econometrically, it should take care of the potential distortion arising from cross-sectional correlation. Substantively, it should account for processes of contagion and competition between countries. Since it is more likely that in the short run income taxes are affected by competition than consumption or payroll taxes, shifts in the tax mix in other countries may affect shifts in the respective country. Modelling spatial interdependence is relatively new to

the field of comparative political economy and hence merits a closer look at what is at stake.

Until recently, empirical studies have neglected the issue of international interdependence, although the issue of strategic interaction and policy diffusion has been clearly on the rise for some time. As Franzese and Hays (2004) point out, most empirical studies have focused on international shocks and measurement of openness, but have not engaged with the strategic interactions between national political responses. Excluding direct interaction between policies of countries where it is present leads to the well-known problem of spatial correlation, that is the section-wise correlation of error terms. This correlation has been merely treated as a problem of inference. If diffusion is sizeable, however, not only standard errors but also coefficients are inflated (ibid.: 30). Hence, ignoring diffusion between countries leads scholars to accept relationships of independent regressors too readily.

A simple way of dealing with these difficulties is to introduce so-called spatial lag variables. These work analogously to temporal lags, that is they use information about the dependent variable from other sections $-i$ to account for the section i. It is less clear, however, what order we should expect to dominate spatial lags. For temporal lags the immediate choice is temporal proximity: the more time passes, the less effect should be visible of past states on the present state. An analogous extension of the spatial analysis would be geographic proximity, as suggested for instance in the literature on gravity models for international trade. The econometric downside of using such variables is their simultaneity bias, since they are in part determined by the values of section i. Simply put, space leads to mutual relationships. Hence, we risk throwing the baby out with the bath water if we trust that other coefficients are insignificant in cases were spatial lags yield strong results. Franzese and Hays show that the bias of omitting spatial lags can be very high, whereas even in small samples when the cross-sectional correlation is not too high, the endogeneity bias of spatial variables using simple ordinary least squares is not overly extreme (Franzese and Hays, 2004: 50). This makes them attractive even when compared to more sophisticated techniques such as two-stage least squares or maximum likelihood estimates.

One could think of weighing bilateral relationships between countries with any kind of indicators that show the degree to which these countries are truly intertwined. In the context of international capital flows both governing and being governed by taxation, geographic models lose some of their bite. Differences in taxation may induce capital flows to very distant regions. Yet, if other variables are used instead of proximity, one is most likely to include endogenous variables in the weighting process. For example, if one was to use dyadic trade or financial flows for weighing the impact of each pair-wise relationship between countries, one would surely meet new problems of endogeneity. If trade or capital flows depend on national differences in taxation, this overemphasizes the role of weighted spatial lags. We would be overly confident of finding effects of international interaction. Using simple geographic distances does not generate such risks.

To calculate the spatial lag I used distance data from CEPII[6] and adjusted them to the needs of spatial econometrics. In particular, I constructed a matrix containing the distance-based weights of $n - 1$ other countries on a the nth country. Weights were row-standardized, so that they add up to 1. Next, I multiplied this matrix with the vector of changes in the dependent variable for a given year. To reduce the in-built endogeneity of this spatial lag, I have chosen to use the changes of the previous year. Hence the indicator must be interpreted as follows: it measures how much the relative importance of income taxes increases or decreases, given that the weighted relative importance of income taxes of the other 19 countries has increased or decreased in the previous year. We can see in the last column of Table 5.2 that there is a negative relationship between the spatial lag and the dependent variable. In other words there is a negative contagion across countries.

Diffusion and international competition effects are necessarily difficult to pin down, since they are dynamically unstable. The genuine pattern of international competition is that some countries are swifter in their adjustment of tax systems to competition than others. The argument has been made that this is the case for smaller countries, more open economies or those with fewer veto players. If this is the case, we should expect overall convergence of tax rates and ratio only in the long, but differentiation in the short run. Given the negative sign of the spatial lag I find, one may interpret contagion in the tax mix along these lines. If the other countries increase income taxation, a given country has an incentive to underbid its partners and diverge in the short run. In other words, part of the reason for shifting towards VAT, for example, may lie in governments' strategies to make production in their countries more attractive. In that respect the results are in line with those of Hettich and Winer (1999) and Chernick (2005).

The properties of spatial econometrics in a setting of pooled aggregate data has yet to be fully investigated. One intricate problem is a potential small sample bias in estimating the coefficient of the spatial lag. To calculate the weights for the other countries, it is standard practice to set the weight of the country under study zero. This reduces the risk of endogeneity. Nevertheless, a variable that is unevenly distributed in a small sample may lead to a regression to the mean, since influential cases will be simply left out of the regression. To neutralize this effect I have done several auxiliary regressions setting arbitrary weights for the respective country and have checked for a bias. In the regression here I found little difference and therefore refrained from reporting these results. A last question is whether I should have used reiterative estimation techniques to account for the endogeneity of the spatial lag. Since its value is still in an acceptable range for Franzese and Hays (2007), and, compared to previous model, the coefficients of the interesting independent variables do not change, I have not followed this strategy.

Endogeneity of unemployment and taxation

The previous results showed no interesting causal relation running from unemployment towards taxation. It is tempting to stop here, but the finding conflicts with those of Chapter 3, in which I have found some effect comparing the three tax forms. Therefore I will bind both findings together and analyse the case for a circular relationship between taxation and unemployment. I will estimate a simple system of two equations and will compare the results of simple OLS estimations with the estimates of three-stage least squares (3SLS). Given the problems of model specification in pooled aggregate data, the following evidence needs to be interpreted with utmost caution.

As in Chapter 3 I have decided against the use of an error-correction model given the lack of robustness. Nevertheless, I need to include some institutional level effects. Therefore, I use a specification with first differences, but include the key variables of interest – taxes and unemployment – also in their first lags. I calculate a simple system of two equations, one for the first temporal difference of the relative importance of income taxation and one for the first temporal difference in unemployment rates. The generic version of this system of equations looks as follows

$$\Delta T = \beta_1 \times \Delta U + \beta_2 \times U_{t-1} + \beta_j \times \Sigma \Delta x_j \qquad (5.1)$$

$$\Delta U = \beta_3 \times \Delta T + \beta_4 \times T_{t-1} + \beta_k \times \Sigma \Delta z_k \qquad (5.2)$$

For Equation 5.1 I take the same dependent variable and the small set of regressors from Model 1 in Table 5.2 and add the spatial lag. For the second equation the first difference of unemployment is the dependent variable and the independent variables are inflation, growth, openness as well as the inequality and the cabinet share of social democrats. Admittedly, the model specification for unemployment could be much more sophisticated, but the selection follows similar politico-economic models of

Table 5.3   Simultaneous equations

	Simultaneous equations			
	3SLS Δ T	3SLS Δ U	OLS Δ T	OLS Δ U
Δ_{t-1} employment protection	−0.013		−0.023	
	(0.015)		(0.018)	
Δ_{t-1} surplus coverage	−0.0015*		−0.0021**	
	(0.00090)		(0.0010)	
Δ Unemployment	−0.043***		0.0000025	
	(0.0034)		(0.0040)	
Lag unemployment	−0.000031		0.00029	
	(0.00067)		(0.00080)	
Δ inflation	0.0036***	−0.029	0.0076***	−0.090***
	(0.0014)	(0.031)	(0.0014)	(0.014)
Δ openness	0.00079	0.014	0.00025	0.0099
	(0.00076)	(0.0096)	(0.00077)	(0.0078)
GDP growth	−0.0043***	−0.17***	0.0062***	−0.21***
	(0.0016)	(0.034)	(0.0017)	(0.017)
Δ_{t-1} spatial lag	−0.11		−0.25*	
	(0.12)		(0.13)	
Δ t1rel		−0.09**		−0.14
		(0.04)		(0.44)
Lag t1rel		0.0080		0.039
		(0.086)		(0.064)
Δ_{t-1} inequality		−5.73***		−7.58***
		(1.76)		(1.43)
Δ social democrats		0.00055		0.00095
		(0.0015)		(0.0015)
Constant	0.018**	0.59***	−0.017**	0.69***
	(0.0071)	(0.088)	(0.0079)	(0.078)
Observations	575	575	575	575
R^2	0.078	0.08	0.107	0.406

Notes:
Levels of significance: * < 0.10, ** < 0.05, *** < 0.01.
Robust standard errors in parentheses, adjusted for small sample size.

unemployment (Iversen, 1999; Mares, 2006). Moreover, the independent variables are chosen to fulfil the necessary requirements of identification in a simultaneous equation system.

Table 5.3 shows the results of a 3SLS-regression and contrasts it with simple OLS estimates. The most important result of this table is that ΔU indeed has a negative impact on the relative weight of income taxes, and that increases in ΔT reduce changes in unemployment rates. There is a case for a mutual dependency in the results of the 3SLS-system. Compared to this we do not find significant relationships of unemployment on taxes or vice versa in the OLS estimates. A Hausman test corroborates the idea that there is a bias of endogeneity in the OLS regressions.[7]

The table shows that there is some evidence for the case that more income taxes relative to other forms of labour taxation do not do harm to the labour market. Controlling for endogeneity we see that a 1 per cent rise in the ratio of income to other taxes leads to a decrease of the unemployment rate by some 0.1 per cent. Shifting towards income taxation is not the sole solution to unemployment, but its importance is nevertheless considerable.

The labour market variables in the tax equation show roughly the same relationships as in the previous table. This also goes for the other independent determinants of taxation. In the OLS equation of unemployment we see the negative coefficients for both inflation and growth that are typical for such regressions (Franz, 1993). Yet inflation loses significance once we go to the simultaneous equation system. As for the other variables, there is only a trade-off visible with inequality (for example Kenworthy, 2003) whereas openness and social democrats do not show any effects in either of the two equations for unemployment.

All in all, we see that there is a case for a mutual dependence between tax systems and the performance of the labour market. On the one hand, the political explanation of evolutions in the tax system remains robust against treating unemployment as an endogenous variable. This is important news: I have used institutional explanations as controls for the endogenous part of taxes and I have distilled a pure effect on unemployment which corroborates the findings of Chapter 3.

QUALITATIVE EVIDENCE

To gain further insights into the political dynamics within the political agent 'labour' I will resort to case-study evidence. The first section will deal with the long-term trends in the German tax structure to show that the political economy approach helps us understanding a fundamental asymmetry in the politics of income taxation: whereas it was treated as a tax on capital and land ownership in the nineteenth century, it is nowadays, by and large, a tax on labour. Given this caveat we will see that Wilhelmine Germany fits the logic presented in the previous sections. Next, I will go on to compare evolutions of the tax structure in the UK and Germany after the Second World War. We will see that intra-class conflicts in the

British Labour Party finally resulted in a thorough break with the past and a resurgence of policies that try to combine more tax progression with lower burden on low-wage employment. In Germany this rupture with the past has been much weaker. As a consequence one can note a stop-and-go policy of burdening and unburdening the low-wage sector. In the comparative case study I will back my observation on the issue of the tax mix with some discussion of functional equivalent means, in particular in the realm of labour market policies.

Revisiting Nineteenth-Century Germany

In the introduction of this book I mentioned Bismarck's worries about a contribution-based scheme of social insurance. Since many scholars treat Wilhelmine Germany as the cradle of the modern welfare state this historical epoch has provoked a large interest (Ritter, 1997; Tennstedt and Winter, 1993; Schmidt, 1998). Wilhelmine Germany has also been frequently used as an empirical example for investigating issues of tax competition and economic integration (Hallerberg, 1996; Mattli, 1999; Brawley, 1997). But the area of overlap has not. Bringing these two perspectives – the evolution of the welfare state and early evidence for tax competition – together we will see how far trade unions and the German Social-democratic Party could shape the tax systems and its progressiveness against severe international and institutional restrictions.

This case study will also illustrate an important caveat when making historical comparisons: I argue that there has been an important causal switch in the role of taxation from the eighteenth to the twentieth century. With respect to the choice of the tax structure, before the expansion of the welfare state the dominant cleavage was within capital, thereafter it was within labour. In some ironic twist the welfare state may have even contributed to this long-term transformation. Correspondingly, Wilhelmine Germany serves as a template to look for similar politico-economic mechanisms working under different contextual factors.

Germany's many tax systems
Hallerberg's (1996) study on German tax competition in the second half of the nineteenth century is an interesting start for my discussion. He argues that the major changes in the tax system before the beginning of the First World War were: (a) an upward convergence in tax levels, in his eyes refuting the argument that tax competition automatically leads to downward pressure; (b) less mobile tax bases were only taxed where political institutions allowed this to be done. Hence property was only slightly taxed in Prussia because of the census franchise, whereas it was taxed more heavily

in southern German states with liberal constitutions. (c) Labour taxation remained lower than would be expected by a tax competition model. Using the framework of Chapter 4 – preferences, restrictions and institutions – I will take up these issues to show why and how labour ended up with seemingly low tax rates.

With the end of the Holy Roman Empire in 1806 economic integration proceeded for several decades before political integration caught up with it. So a first remark has to be made about the starting point when delineating tax competition, which arguably precedes German unification in 1870. Negotiations on economic liberalization between German states started soon after Napoleon's defeat in 1815. They led to the formation of a tariff union (*Zollunion*) in 1834 and culminated in the German empire of 1870.

The empire consisted of 25 very heterogeneous states all with different systems of taxation. Across levels there was a system of mixed financing. Indirect taxes were partly pooled at the central level, and mainly consisted of tariffs and specific excise taxes (Henning, 1996: 622). Most direct taxes remained at the state level (Hallerberg, 1996). The Reich mirrored the tax mix of other federal countries at that time, such as Switzerland or the US (Wehler, 1995: 885). The tax base with the least mobility, land or property taxes, was an important public revenue source in many German states, and was politically a more salient issue than nowadays. For this reason German states were reluctant to pool these taxes at the central level. In the 1880s, the introduction of a social security system led to the accumulation of specifically earmarked public revenue in the form of social security contributions, but its size was for a long time marginal. On the central level a genuine income tax was only introduced in 1913. This stands in marked contrast to a country such as Britain, where some form of income taxation had already been introduced in the late eighteenth century as a means to finance the war against Napoleon (O'Brien, 1988).

In a non-democratic regime one has to be careful what kind of political cleavages and interests constitute the polity. The German Empire was a political federation dominated by one player: Prussia. So we have to inspect this player more closely. Historians hold two distinct and somewhat conflicting beliefs about the Prussian state (Steinmetz, 2000). They argue either that it was an autocratic regime with substantial autonomy *vis-à-vis* the society (Skocpol cited in Steinmetz, 2000: 265) or that it was a state largely controlled by the old feudal 'Junker' class of land-owning aristocrats (Taylor, 2004). Hallerberg implicitly uses both notions. He argues that the upward convergence of tax levels was mainly due to the fact that the Prussian government needed higher revenues, while the other countries followed the 'Stackelberg leader' (Hallerberg, 1996: 349). The fact that property taxes were left mostly untouched was, in his view, due to the political resistance of land-owners, who were privileged in their political representation. According to this reading the endurance of agrarian interests in Germany is part of the German 'Sonderweg'. This is true in that the German state was autocratic, but it underestimates the role of the business sector and of influential branches such as iron and steel in the German system.

The role of business

Hallerberg argues that taxes on capital were higher than the conventional race to the bottom story would suggest. But once you look at the whole 'package' taxation, trade policy and public subsidies, it becomes clear that political deals struck between industrialists and agrarians were in the mutual interest of both. In the case of nineteenth-century Canada, Hettich and Winer (1999, Chapter 10) show that the tax structure depended on the level of tariffs imposed on imports. A similar interdependence was visible in the German case. Although higher tariffs were an instrument that clearly favoured agrarians, they were not necessarily harmful for influential German companies (Henning, 1996: 810). Instead, companies shifted higher tariffs forward on to consumers who bore the brunt of protectionism. Industrialists benefited from the subsidies they received for building railways and, after 1900, the German navy (Taylor, 2004: 176). The industrialists maximized the net benefits of this package deal, by agreeing to comparatively high levels of taxation, which were then compensated by these subsidies (see also Tilly, 1966).

Data on the total level of subsidies towards the business sector is difficult to gather, but some estimates illustrate the idea that taxes net of subsidies and public contracts were much lower. During the nineteenth and early twentieth centuries the major item in public outlays was public defence, which benefited the German metal and steel industry (Henning, 1996: 1085). In contrast, even at the eve of the First World War social expenditure was a mere 3 per cent of the public budget. Moreover, this is only the public budget itself and does not include other forms of subsidies, such as the special royalties granted to railways. It is therefore a plausible assumption that industrialists knew how to flex their political muscle and yielded a net benefit even if this did not show up in lower levels of taxation for them.

In a similar vein, recent historical research emphasizes the fact that industrialists also shaped early social policies very much to their liking (Steinmetz, 2000: 265). Before the First World War German social policy was largely a set of 'poor laws' (Lindert, 2004) and the social insurance transfers did not outgrow means-tested benefits during this period. Business also played a strong role in the decision for a contribution-based system of social security. Again one has to be careful not to confound nominal with real incidence of the burden. Ullmann (cited in Lindert, 2004: 174), for instance, argues that big industry was very swift with rolling the burden of contribution on to consumers, whereas small export-oriented firms largely opposed social insurance. In a remarkable resonance of Przeworski and Wallerstein (1988), Steinmetz (2000: 301) conclude that the autocratic Prussian state was largely dependent on 'big' capital and was not able to act contrary to its interests.

The role of labour

Given this reading a new question arises: Why was labour not taxed more heavily at that time? This brings us back to an analysis of the economic and political restrictions.

Hallerberg largely talks about the mobility of a tax base and concludes that more mobile taxes, such as taxes on companies, were not less taxed than less mobile taxes such as those on property. Labour was not taxed extensively, according to Hallerberg, because the German Empire allowed for freedom of settlement which increased labour mobility. But inter-state mobility was a minor cause for a high elasticity of labour taxes. A more important one was whether the tax base was large enough to be taxable at all. Indeed, absolute tax bases were so small that most eighteenth-century (political) economists such as David Ricardo assumed that the incidence of total taxation fell exclusively on capital (Krugman and Obstfeld, 1997: 59). Today's labour economists argue largely the opposite (see Chapter 3). This leaves us with the idea that labour taxation could only become a political issue with the development of the welfare state, and the concomitant growth of a 'taxable' tax basis: real wages.

Indeed German pauperism peaked in about 1850 (Henning, 1996: 749) and real income only surpassed its level of 1780 some 90 years later (ibid.: 1096), around the time when the second German Empire was founded. The level of real wages was not very much higher than the reproductive wage, that is the wage a worker needed for his basic needs. It was at times even lower, as the numerous famines of the period serve to remind us (Fogel, 1990). It is therefore no wonder that real wages only started to grow substantively in the last quarter of the nineteenth century. Figure 5.1 shows some consensus estimates for the evolution of real wages from 1820 to 1920 in Germany and compares them to the real wages in Great Britain.[8] Even in Great Britain, the pioneer of industrial revolution, real wages took off comparatively late, from the 1840s onwards. Analysing wage data of British craftsmen Clark (2005) concludes that till the middle of the nineteenth century the medieval trend of a Malthusian society was still followed in which population growth determines real wages. He continues arguing (p. 1319):

> David Ricardo's adoption and elaboration of the subsistence wage doctrine in the Principals of Political Economy and Taxation published in 1817 were also entirely reasonable at the time of its formulation, given the path of real wages to that point.

Under these circumstances, in the first half of the nineteenth century taxing wages was not a feasible strategy for any government. What happened thereafter? To answer this question it is important to see that it is the relative elasticity of both sides of the market that counts for the incidence of taxation. In the second half of the nineteenth century, the balance was tipped more and more in favour of labour supply. There were several reasons for this. The demographic explosion had already reached its high-point in the early eighteenth century, so that growth rates slowed down when the economic integration process started. Labour supply continued to increase in the middle of the nineteenth century, but at a slower rate (Henning, 1996: 296). Labour demand, however, increased dramatically after major technical innovations made workers in the manufacturing sector scarce.

More importantly, a factor that worked against the taxation of labour was the organization of labour itself. The lower panel of Figure 5.1 shows the evolution of union membership and the number of strikes in the nineteenth century, again for Germany and the UK compared.[9] Although both strikes and union membership were subject to business cycles there is a clear upward trend visible in both countries. Until the First World War union density approached 25 per cent in Great Britain and 15 per cent in Germany. There is also evidence that in both countries unions replaced strong measures such as strikes with more moderate strategies of negotiation and collective bargaining (Cronin, 1984: 107). A comparison of both panels in Figure 5.1 also shows a roughly similar upward trend in union members and real wages. Needless to say that increases in real wages depended on many more factors than strong unions, but many economic historians would argue that it played an important role at the time (Desai, 1968; Brey, 1960).

Since I am also interested in the heterogeneity of labour, not only its strength, it is also important to look at the composition of trade unions. Again Germany mirrored earlier evolutions in British trade unions (Cronin, 1984: 83). The first workers to get organized were typically higher skilled craftsmen (Ritter, 1963: 110), but until the First World War unionism became increasingly a mass phenomenon and the median union member was much more low-skilled than before (Ritter, 1963: 113). Hence, unions

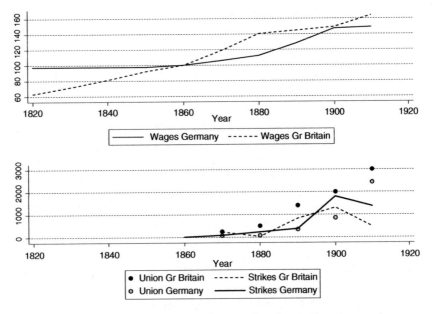

*Figure 5.1   Real wages, union members and strikes in the nineteenth
            century*

became more and more encompassing, but they did not 'over-represent'
insiders since extension clauses of collective wage bargaining or other
labour market institutions that drive wedges between workers were absent.
In fact, the institutionalization of employment protection and collective
bargaining was a product of the Weimar Republic (Alber, 1982).

From the very beginning German trade unions and the labour movement had political motives (Ritter, 1963: 13). Taxation became an important part of its political programme. In the Communist Manifest Marx
(1989 [1848]) himself argued for high tax progression. Similar claims soon
pervaded both trade union publications and those of their political ally:
the Social Democrats. Fearing a socialist revolution, Bismarck used a
twin strategy of prohibiting workers' associations and granting some of
their political demands such as social security (Ritter, 1963: 27). This did
weaken the course of the labour movement, but only for some time. With
the Gotha programme of 1875 the Social Democrats explicitly referred to
a progressive income tax (Corneo, 2005: 17) and henceforth fought for its
introduction.

This pressure was not without consequences: Some smaller German
states introduced an income tax from 1848 on. Prussia introduced a
(minor) income tax in 1893, and the German Reich did so in 1913. But

both the timing and scope of these income taxes show that the political institutions hampered labour interests. Hallerberg (1996) shows that the tax mix depended on political institutions such as the franchise. In states like Prussia the ancien régime had a tight grip on legislation because of a class-based franchise that gave more power to the rich. Here it was particularly difficult to implement progressive tax forms such as income taxation. Also for elections to the Reichstag (national parliament) the voting rules worked against the Social Democrats. The plurality rule and the design of constituencies led to the fact that Social Democrats received significantly fewer seats in parliament than votes (Ritter, 1963: 67).

Finally, it is noteworthy that the conservatives as the major opponents of labour were against the introduction of a modern income tax. Bismarck himself dreaded such a tax at either state or federal level for its sheer redistributive potential: 'eine rationelle Begrenzung des Prinzips der progressiven Besteuerung ist nicht möglich, dasselbe entwickelt sich, einmal rechtlich anerkannt, weiter in der Richtung, in welcher die Ideale des Sozialismus liegen' (quoted in Henning, 1996: 886).[10] This shows that a progressive income tax clearly polarized the electorate between conservative, rich voters and left, poor voters.

Conclusions

Where does this lead our discussion? The general picture is that historical comparisons are insightful but sometimes deceiving. Even if a non-democratic state tends to exhibit a leviathan-type behaviour, it needs the backing of powerful classes. This also holds when exit strategies are not feasible, as long as these classes can voice their interests (Brawley, 1997). This was the case for the industrialists of turn-of-the-century Germany. The tax mix could neither easily be shifted to the shoulders of employees, since the tax base of real wages was small and the political resilience of workers grew stronger. This drives home our idea that the welfare state (and the wage-bargaining system) are influential institutions for the impact that taxes have on the labour market: one needs some degree of 'decommodification' in the parlance of Esping-Andersen (1990) to make labour face the burden of taxation effectively. With no welfare state, no wage-bargaining institutions and low real wages, the only way to tax labour is consumption. This was exactly what happened back then. Nowadays taxation falls overwhelmingly on labour: income, payroll and consumption taxes. In that sense decisions on tax policies today are not really comparable with that of 100 years ago.

In the following we will see that the changing context has also visible implications for the strategic options of the political left. When income taxation was about expropriating the rich, it was unambiguously preferred by trade unions and left political parties, as the German example shows.

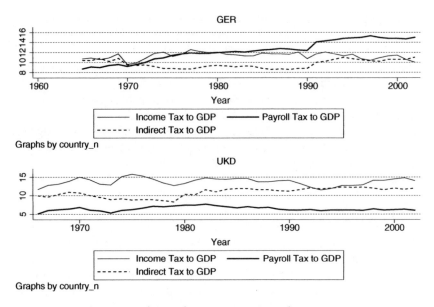

Figure 5.2   German and British tax mix compared

For the period after the Second World War, this pattern is not so clear any more.

Comparative Evidence on Germany and the UK

Let us start with a look at aggregate statistics of tax ratios. Figure 5.2 shows the evolution of the tax mix in Germany and the UK after the Second World War.[11] In Germany income tax ratios peaked in the late 1970s and went on an almost continuous decline thereafter. Economic shocks such as the oil crises and reunification led to noticeable jumps of social security contributions. From the 1980s onwards payroll taxes became the dominant form of public revenues, but indirect taxes in the form of VAT has caught up in recent years. In the UK the income tax ratio hit its all-time high in the mid 1970s, became briefly more important in the early Thatcher years, and then went back into decline until the mid-1990s. Since then income tax revenues have recovered slightly. Indirect tax revenues have increased over the whole period. Only during the Labour governments of the late 1960s and 1970s was payroll taxation of some importance.

In both countries one sees influences of business cycles (inflation and growth) in the growth of income tax. This corresponds to our previous quantitative findings. One can also see long term changes that are due

Table 5.4   Comparison of Tax Schedules

	Year	Basic allowance	Lowest rate (%)	Highest rate (%)
	Nominal Tax Rates – UK and Germany			
Germany				
	1971	2430	19	54.59
	1981	1839	22	56
	1991	3766	13	53
	2005	7665	15	45
UK				
	1971	20,939	38.75	88.75
	1981	8690	30	60
	1991	7156	25	40
	2005	7119	10	40

Note: Basic allowances/zero zone in Euros 2005, ppp-adjusted.

Source: Own calculations on basis of OECD and BMF (various years).

more to political than economic reasons that shift the tax mix away from progression. Of course, higher income taxes do not automatically lead to higher levels of progressivity (see Chapter 2) and yet different measures of tax-based redistribution move broadly in line with ratios in both countries. Table 5.4 shows changes in the basic allowances (in constant prices) and the lowest and highest statutory tax rates of the income tax code over time. For Germany one sees no clear trend for lower incomes, but a downward trend on top income rates. Using both statutory marginal rates and coefficients of 'residual progression' Corneo (2005) shows for Germany that from 1958 till the mid-1980s tax progression was on the rise for middle and high incomes, whereas it has decreased from then on. Very low incomes of half the average GDP per capita income, have seen a remarkable increase in marginal rates so that the overall progressivity of highest and lowest income brackets has been reduced since the mid-1970s.

In the UK one sees a similar pattern. After a steady increase of progressivity till the first oil crisis, it declines dramatically during the Thatcher years. Even more than in Germany the decrease is due to changes in the tax system (Johnson and Webb, 1993). As Table 5.4 shows the threshold for the first tax rates shrank dramatically, and the distance between first and highest statutory rates decreased. In recent years the tax schedule has become slightly more progressive again, but its impact on overall income inequality has been limited so far (Brewer *et al.*, 2007).

The comparative picture becomes even sharper if we look beyond the tax structure into adjacent areas of labour market policies. Functional equivalents to tax progressivity are targeted subsidies, in-work benefits and welfare-to-work programmes. In close correspondence to the overall evolution of the tax structure these targeted programmes show cross-country variation: whereas in the UK the family credit has been continually expanded, the deep divisions within the German left in interaction with the complicated political institutions have led to 'stop and go' reform policies.

The aim of this section is to investigate the political reasons for these evolutions focusing again on the role of trade unions and workers' parties. We will see that in both countries there was similar tension within the workforce during the economic turmoil of the 1970s and early 1980s, but that the outcome of these tensions are different: whereas old traditional labour was fundamentally weakened in the UK of Margaret Thatcher, German trade unions were hit by the disastrous aftermaths of reunification. Compared with the British case this blow against unionism was later and affected the economic role more than the political role of unions. This has had consequences for the progressivity of the tax mix. Recent Labour governments in the UK have managed to reintroduce some degree of progressivity, whereas in Germany it is still on the decline.

The rise of income taxation until late 1970s
The period from the end of the Second World War till the late 1970s is the golden age of income taxation in both countries. Not only were income taxes the major tax form, but also they became more and more progressive. This correlates with a strong political representation of unions and left parties (Garrett, 1998). In both countries unions had close ties to major political parties and were directly inserted into the corporatist arrangement of the state. However, sectoral changes were under way that deeply changed the composition and the scope of trade unions in these three decades. With it came the first signs of a roll-back in the progressivity of the tax mix.

As mentioned earlier, German income taxation was introduced comparatively late. Only in the Weimar Republic did Germany replace the 27 income taxes on the state level by a national income tax, but social security contributions were of much greater (political) importance as sources of revenue (Lindert, 2004). Military occupation after 1945, however, gave income taxation a big push since the Allied Forces installed a very progressive scheme with marginal rates as high as 95 per cent.

The first democratically elected government of Konrad Adenauer cut general levels of taxation to stimulate economic activity (Zohlnhöfer, 2006). It was very careful, however, to maintain or even increase tax progression. This was in part the consequence of the ideological closeness to the Catholic church (Manow, 2002), but it also had a clear strategic component: Adenauer's party, the Christian-Democratic Union (CDU), aimed at the centre of the political spectrum and at integrating workers into its electorate. Hence, its political future depended directly on the permissive consensus of trade unions which the CDU tried to lure with tax policies, but also with measures that strengthened the role of trade unions in big companies such as workers' councils and codetermination (Zohlnhöfer, 2006: 8). The Adenauer government also sowed the seeds for the latter explosion of social security contributions: it linked pension benefits to economic growth and introduced new benefits such as schemes for early retirement (Trampusch, 2005; Manow and Seils, 2000).

With the first postwar economic crisis Social Democrats came into office, first as the smaller coalition partner of the CDU in 1966, then as the dominant political force in a social-liberal coalition government from 1969 onwards. The political change also marked a change towards Keynesian economic policy. Fighting the economic crisis eventually made higher revenues necessary. Automatic adjustment kicked in and increased social security contributions enormously (Manow and Seils, 2000). At the same time, the government depended on the wage restraint of trade unions and enhanced efforts to insert unions directly in the so-called Konzertierte Aktion (Scharpf, 1987), a tripartite corporatist arrangement. The result of this process was a high point in union power. In 1969 the Social Democrats won the elections, not least due to support from trade unions. Union density still increased and unions proved their militancy in a number of wildcat strikes in the early 1970s even before the oil crisis changed the political tug of war decisively (Schmid, 2006).

The mid-1970s mark a turning point in the representativeness of trade unions. Bargaining coverage was instituted already in the Weimar years, but the German constitution or Basic Law (Art. 9,3) strengthened unions with the freedom of workers' associations to bargain for wages autonomously. Increases of union density narrowed the gap to bargaining coverage to less than 60 per cent until 1975; thereafter, bargaining coverage continued to increase slightly whereas union density started to decline. The rise in union power concealed a qualitative change in union membership. The median union member represented more and more medium-skilled workers, most importantly of big companies, which themselves rationalized their workforce by shedding the lower-skilled (Carruth and Schnabel, 1990).

Unions, sometimes in coalition with employers' associations, demanded new policies such as the expansion of early retirement schemes (Trampusch, 2005) notwithstanding the sharp rise in social security contributions these measures provoked. The political demands started to mirror this shift in composition since early retirement or higher unemployment benefits were predominantly in the interest of the core of the workforce. Moreover, wage negotiations and the expansion of the social wage should act as a whip for employers to increase productivity (Scharpf, 1987). This pattern eventually affected tax policy: if the strategy of social partners is to enhance productivity, it is not reasonable to 'subsidize' low-wage workers by tax progression. The issue of tax progressivity became one about taxing the highest income brackets, not all across the income range.

Compared with the German Reich, British governments experimented very early with modern income taxes. Income taxes were first introduced to finance the English war against France (O'Brien, 1988). Income taxation finally took off in the early twentieth century and became more and more progressive (Daunton, 2002). From its beginning the Labour Party and the trade unions backed financing the welfare state out of (income) tax revenue (ibid.: 265). In contrast, payroll taxes have always remained a secondary source of public revenues. This is primarily due to the tax-based funding of the Beveridge welfare state. The Treasury, which traditionally played a strong and autonomous role in the formation of tax policies (Daunton, 2002: 18), was against payroll or indirect taxation due to their regressive nature (Steinmo, 1993: 106). Even before the Second World War it was clear that increases in taxation were only possible, if unions were inserted to the administration of welfare benefits (Daunton, 2002: 48). Since unions also preferred taxation as opposed to contributions, this implied that the expansion of the welfare state was, by and large, based on taxation. It is therefore somewhat ironic that Beveridge endorsed contribution-based financing of flat-rate benefits (Daunton, 2002: 309), whereas Bismarck had proposed a tax-based scheme, and both of these plans failed.

Early after the Second World War, governments sought the consent of trade unions and engaged in corporatist brokering in tax policy (Daunton, 2002). Unions made their consent dependent on the extension of tax progression to wealth taxation (ibid.: 200). Both Tory and Labour governments had to respect these wishes or otherwise faced dire consequences. For example, the Conservative Chancellor of the Exchequer, Peter Thorneycroft, resigned in 1958 as a result of tensions with trade unions and their demands for higher public spending (Daunton, 2002: 274). For tax policies, the strong influence of redistributive demands meant that top marginal rates sky-rocketed to 98 per cent. Alternatives there were few, since Labour staunchly rejected any attempts to increase indirect taxation (Daunton, 2002: 208).

The Conservative governments of Eden, Macmillan and Douglas-Home managed to lower public spending and statutory tax rates somewhat. They also undermined tax progression by granting tax rebates to elderly and house owners (ibid.: 282). With the next Labour government of Harold Wilson higher spending was once again on the political agenda. In the quest for new sources of revenue the Labour government of Wilson fatally experimented with a selective employment tax. This tax epitomizes most of the claims made in this book: it is a direct levy on employment with a comparatively narrow tax base, it was supported by the trade unions,[12] and one of its major motives was to crowd out employment in sectors with low productivity such as hotels and retail services. Given both its unpopularity and inefficiency its life span was short. Labour's attempts to replace it by a general payroll tax applying to all forms of wage income came too late. The next incoming Conservative government under Edward Heath replaced it with VAT in 1973, a move which was also in line with the imminent UK accession to the European Communities (Kato, 2003). The introduction of VAT was accompanied by a major tax relief to rich people and further decreased the overall progressivity of the tax system.

Heath's government also tried to reform trade unionism and to fight its growing militancy, but trade unions remained victorious. The energy shortages in the aftermath of strikes organized by the National Union of Mineworkers added much to the demise of the Tory government in 1974. Despite its closer contacts with the union, the next Labour government under James Callaghan did not fare any better. Macroeconomic imbalances were such that tax policy decisions were severely impeded. To combat high inflation and unemployment, Callaghan demanded wage restraint from unions, which they rejected (Scharpf, 1987). The confrontation led to the notorious winter of discontent and the ushering in of a new period of tax policy under Margaret Thatcher.

A look at the structural conditions of union membership shows the growing political power of unions until the late 1970s. Not least due to the political confrontation, membership rates increased until 1979 whereas attempts to curtail their power and scope of influence were, by and large ineffective. However, as in the German case, the peak in union membership masks some of the qualitative changes in the composition of unions from the 1960s onwards. Trade unions attracted an increasing number of white collar workers for whom tax progression was less appealing (Daunton, 2002: 336). Deindustrialization was clearly under way (Kemmerling, 2003). With these changes came changes in the politics of income taxation: Labour was less clear in its endorsement of higher tax progression and the resistance towards proportional or even regressive taxes (Daunton, 2002: 338).

Conservative retrenchment of tax progression in the 1980s
In the late 1970s and early 1980s economic crises led to the demise of left governments in both countries. In both cases this also led to major reforms

that made public revenues less progressive. In the case of the United Kingdom Margaret Thatcher's radical ideology takes much of the blame for this evolution (Pierson, 1994; Rhodes, 2000). Thatcher was careful not only to implement tax reforms but also to cut union power as she considered unions to be her major political enemies. In the German case the explanation is more puzzling, since the Kohl government's position on tax and social issues was not so far away from the Social Democrats.[13] Moreover, it crucially depended on some level of consensus with trade unions on issues of labour market and social reforms (Schmidt, 1998; Scharpf, 1987). If tax policy changed in this period it must have been because of hard economic restraints or because the Social Democrats and the trade unions were not so firmly aligned behind the idea of tax progression any more.

In 1982 the Kohl government came with the promise of a 'moral turnaround' which put the blame for a stagnant economy, comparatively high rates of unemployment and increasing budget deficits on Social Democratic policy making. In the beginning, the government opted for an austerity package that included some cuts in welfare benefits (Scharpf, 1987). In the Budget Reform Act of 1983 the Kohl government increased VAT and social security contributions (Zohlnhöfer, 2006). To counterbalance the regressive impact somewhat the government also decreased family allowances for very rich people. Having achieved a mild budget consolidation, the Kohl government went on to reform the tax system in three steps from 1986 to 1990. The revenue effects of this reform were fairly small. Both the top marginal rate and the lowest rate were cut slightly, and basic allowance was mildly increased. In effective terms, the tax reforms mainly benefited the middle class (Ganghof, 2004: 68). Taken together, Kohl's tax policy was not very much different from tax policies of his Social Democratic predecessor.

This also holds for the expenditure side of the budget. The Kohl government was not very successful in cutting benefits. In 1984 it reduced unemployment benefits and unemployment assistance slightly, but at the same time it increased eligibility for earnings-related unemployment benefits to 32 months (Zohlnhöfer, 2001: 665). It also increased spending for active labour market policies so that overall contribution to unemployment insurance had to increase slightly over time to keep the budget of the federal employment agency balanced. More importantly for the long-term evolution of the tax mix were decisions to decrease tensions on the labour market with a reduction in labour supply: sending home foreign workers, early retirement and a tax policy that was oriented to the male breadwinner (Schmid, 2006). All these measures led to automatic shifts of the tax mix towards payroll taxation in times of high unemployment (Manow and Seils, 2000).

This became dramatically evident after German reunification. The steep incline in the number of unemployed people and pensioners led to an enormous jump in payroll taxation. Eventually, this made deep cuts in the generosity of welfare benefits necessary, but Social Democrats and trade unions opposed such measures. And yet reunification started to change the underlying political bargains between trade unions and the political parties.

In the 1980s the Kohl government tried to restrict union power somewhat, for instance in its regulation of worker councils, but, in general, reforms of labour market institutions took place at the fringes of the labour market and not in its centre (Zohlnhöfer, 2001: 667). For example, the Kohl government eased the use of limited contracts, but left general employment protection legislation untouched. Neither could the government directly affect the bargaining coverage of trade unions which stayed at high levels throughout the decade, whereas union membership was in decline. With reunification the gap briefly widened as trade unions were not very popular in the formerly communist Eastern Germany, but western unions were successful at exporting labour market regulation to Eastern Germany (Sinn and Sinn, 1992). The unions themselves preferred a wage policy that should lead to a quick levelling of the wage gap by increasing eastern wages to the western standard. The idea was once again to force productivity levels to such levels that growth and consumption would kick in (Sinn and Sinn, 1992). As a result unions' wage policies added to the major slump in employment that was already on its way because of the economic transformation.

Facing this pressure the later years of the Kohl government resulted in a continuous struggle against high labour costs. The government had to introduce a new 'solidarity' surcharge on income taxes, and yet the relative proportion of income taxation went down, since the inflow of unemployed and retired Eastern Germans led to a steep incline of contribution rates. In its last years the Kohl government aimed at a major tax reform, the so-called Petersberger proposal, which, for example, would have cut top marginal income taxes from 53 to 39 per cent. The Social Democrats, who dominated the second chamber in the parliament, refused to accept this proposal.[14] With their veto the most important income tax reform of the Kohl government failed. However, there was one factor that re-established some degree of progression on the lower end of the income scale. In an influential ruling the German Federal Court of Justice demanded in 1995 a dramatic increase of the basic allowances in income taxation. It argued that the basic allowance had to be in line with the social minimum of the social security system. The government had to respond with a twofold increase of basic allowances (see Table 5.4).

To summarize, we see that the conservative government did not implement very far reaching policy reforms against the interest of unions and Social Democrats. If the tax mix shifted towards less progressivity this was due to automatic adjustment against which neither the conservatives nor a heterogeneous and indecisive left fought strongly.

Compared with German tax reforms, the Thatcher government implemented radical solutions. In the first three years the government cut both the highest and lowest income tax rate, and it also decreased basic allowance so that the lowest incomes had to pay higher taxes after the reform. More importantly, she increased VAT from 8 to 12.5 per cent and did not act against fiscal drag in the course of high inflation. On the expenditure side, Thatcher did not bring down overall spending because of high unemployment, but generosity clearly fell (Rhodes, 2000). She made welfare benefits liable to income taxation and cut replacement rates of unemployment and pension benefits (Pierson, 1994: 59).

Moreover, the Thatcher government immediately confronted trade unions. The winter of discontent had driven a wedge between trade unions and public opinion, especially once strikes became violent (Towers, 1989). Thatcher used this window of opportunity to implement several complementary measures: she prohibited the use of so-called flying pickets and closed shops which tapped into the organizational capabilities of the trade unions directly. She also revised the legal status of trade unions and tried to cut unions' donations to the Labour party (Pinto-Duschinsky, 1989). But her fiercest weapon was privatization. As a measure against the militant miners' union, she closed many pits and sold off the rest of them. Rising unemployment hit union density fatally. Taken together her measures successfully aimed at the heart of British trade unionism. It is also remarkable to note that since union density was already in decline from the mid-1970s, her measures strongly reduced the gap between bargaining coverage and union density so that unions are not only weaker, but their economic influence has mirrored more closely their political influence ever since.

Thatcher's rhetoric was to reduce the size of the public sector and it is well-known that her retrenchment was not very successful at that (Pierson, 1994). And yet, as most observers would say she changed the nature of government and made society less egalitarian. This is clearly visible in her tax policy. The income tax schedule became much less progressive and the mix tilted more and more towards VAT. Rising inequality was a clear result of this tax policy (Johnson and Webb, 1993). Ironically, tax policy was also the reason why she had to resign. When the Thatcher government decided to introduce a flat-rate community charge, the so-called poll tax, it was to decrease the spending behaviour of municipalities. This strategy seriously backfired, since local governments put the blame on the national policy and voters deeply resented a head tax (for example Boix, 1998: 196).

The incoming Major government had to remove the poll tax as quickly as possible. It recurred to VAT which now rose to 17.5 per cent. Major also froze the basic allowance and increased National Insurance Contributions. Hence, Major followed the previous government in its shift towards regressive taxation. However, Major also moved back somewhat to the political centre and increased public spending on education and health. In employment policies the government significantly expanded the in-work benefit scheme 'Family Credit' which had been introduced by the previous administration (Dilnot and McCrae, 2000). And yet, the Major government continued its predecessor's tough stance on employment protection and union power (Rueda, 2006). This middle course between the administration and alternation of the Thatcher heritage proved to be a lame compromise in the eyes of many voters. And voters had an alternative in the form of a fundamentally reinvigorated though transformed Labour Party.

Left governments and tax policy at the turn of the century
The last decade is too short and too recent to be fully analysed here. Many policy reforms linked to taxation are still very much in flux, some are already rolled back again. Nevertheless, there is an interesting contrast to the previous episodes: Labour governments have returned to power, but the nature of these left governments has changed in both countries. The break with the past was much stronger in the UK where we also see some, albeit very weak, signs of a recovery in tax progressivity. In Germany tax and employment policy follow a stop-and-go pattern since the Social Democrats still sway between different ideologies with no clear winner visible so far.

In 1998 Gerhard Schröder broke the spell of four consecutive electoral defeats and ushered in a red–green coalition government. The coalition agreement of both parties promised greater social justice. In the area of tax policy it mentioned the rise in the basic allowances and a lower first rate in the income tax system. Yet this proved to be a minor issue compared with the impending need to adjust the system of corporate and personal income taxation to the needs of a global market.

In the beginning the new government undid some of the reforms undertaken by its predecessor: for example, it undid Kohl's last pension reform and increased pension benefits and it tightened employment protection after the Kohl government had loosened it somewhat. It also made so-called minor jobs of 630 DM (see Chapter 4) liable to social insurance contributions. These reforms did not last for long, however, since the government soon started to take all of these policy reversals back (Egle and Zohlnhöfer, 2007). More importantly, it designed a reform package that included relatively tough austerity measures with a tax reform that cut statutory rates on corporate and personal income dramatically.

The ironic twist of this tax reform was that it came fairly close to the last reform proposal of the Kohl government which the Social Democrats' majority faction of the second chamber had vetoed. From the mid-1990s onward the major political parties perceived tax competition on corporate income to be more and more a serious obstacle to economic growth in Germany (Ganghof, 2004). Since both coalition partners accepted the need for a cut in corporate tax rates, the question remained whether the reform should also include a cut of statutory rates on personal income. Given the complexity of the German income tax systems it was very difficult to find compromises in that respect. Perhaps of even higher importance was the role of the Federal Court of Justice since many politicians rightfully feared the court would veto a tax reform that generated a large gap between corporate and personal income tax rates and thereby violated 'horizontal' tax equity (Ganghof, 2004). The upshot of this veto position was that the corporate tax rate cut from 52 per cent to 39 per cent had to be accompanied by a similar cut in personal rates gradually from 53 to 42 per cent. Counteractive measures to re-establish progressivity were much weaker. The tax reform contained a cut in the first tax rate from 23 to 15 per cent and an increase in the basic allowance, but all things considered, the reform flattened the German income tax schedule to a degree hitherto unknown.

Yet the tax reform, no matter how inefficient or unfair, was of minor political importance compared with the reforms of the labour market and social policies in the so-called Agenda 2010. Reunification had increased the number of unemployed steadily to 4.5 million or 12 per cent of the labour force in 1997. The government promised to tackle this problem, but did not do much about it in the first years so that voters became increasingly disappointed (Egle and Zohlnhöfer, 2007). A scandal in the Federal Employment Agency[15] provided a window of opportunity to finally engage with the reform of the labour market. The result was a package of several reforms, named after the government's key broker Peter Hartz and implemented in the years 2003 to 2005. This reform went far beyond a mere reform of placement services and included a serious cut in benefits for long-term unemployed (Kemmerling and Bruttel, 2006). On the revenue side the reform implied lower contributions to unemployment insurance and a shift in the financing of long-term unemployed into general taxation.

The reform package also included some welfare-to-work policies. Until the reform there were only scattered experiments with in-work benefits in some of the federal states and with very low tax incentives. For instance, the so-called Mainzer Modell gave a tax credit to reduce social security contributions and an increase in child benefits to needy low-wage earners with families. These reductions amounted to some 2 to 5 per cent of the wage of an average production worker (OECD, 2005: 142). The Hartz reform increased the number of subsidies for the low-wage sector and thereby also reduced the taxation of minor jobs. It cautiously expanded the wage range for which the reduction of social security contributions is applicable, promoted 'micro' self-employment, and increased incentives of unemployed to combine benefits with small jobs (Kemmerling and Bruttel, 2006).

It is still very much debated whether some of these reforms added to the recent recovery of the German labour market (for example Bundestag, 2006). Politically the reform proved to be disastrous, since the population deeply resented the retrenchment part of Hartz. Trade unions, the extreme left and non-governmental organizations mobilized against the reform and, in particular, against the subsidies for the low-wage sector, since they feared that the thereby generated jobs would threaten existent jobs. The disruption between the Social Democratic government and the unions led so far that two years after its successful re-election the government resigned and called for new elections which took place in 2005.

All in all, the tax and employment policies of the red–green government were marked by its stop-and-go character: the swing to the left was abruptly halted and the following years saw a moderate degree of deregulation in the labour market and a steep decline of (statutory) tax progression. External economic restrictions in the form of tax competition, and maybe even the European Monetary Union, explain this reversal to some extent, but this explanation is not sufficient. If it is really true that the case for a progressive income tax is more and more difficult to make, left politicians could have still resorted to a functional equivalent: implementing a level of progression in the system of social security contributions (Scharpf, 1995). However, the fiercest opponents of such a strategy came from within labour: traditional Social Democrats and trade unions (Heinze and Streeck, 2003).

For a deeper understanding of these political tensions one has to look at the underlying fissures within the Social Democrats (Egle and Zohlnhöfer, 2007: 9) and their relation to the trade unions. Because of the huge structural changes and the reunification union membership declined steeply in this period. This ultimately also affected the economic and political bargaining power of unions, but with a considerable time lag. Once Schröder made it obvious that he held 'Blairism' and new Labour in high esteem (Schröder and Blair, 1999; Glyn and Wood, 2001) unions became alarmed. Unlike in the UK the estrangement of the Social Democrats and the trade unions harmed Schröder more seriously. One reason was that despite its decline in membership German unions were still much more powerful than in the UK. This is due to the institutional entrenchment of trade union-ism in the welfare state and the constitution. A second important reason lies in the German electoral system. Unlike in the UK the proportional system always allows for minor but more radical left parties to compete against the Social Democrats. This was already visible in the 1980s when the Greens seized some of the left domain (Kitschelt, 1994), and it became once more obvious after reunification and, in particular, after the Hartz laws when the ex-communist party of Eastern Germany got a grip on the West German electorate. The existence of political alternatives puts the unions in a stronger position *vis-à-vis* the Social Democrats.

This was very different in the case of British Labour. Already in his elec-toral campaign Tony Blair made sure that he would not revert to Labour's previous positions on tax and redistributive policies. In particular, he promised not to raise income tax rates. He kept his promises, but during his government income tax revenues and effective rates began to rise again, a policy the opposition denounced as 'taxation by stealth'. New Labour also reintroduced some degree of progression, albeit on a much lower absolute level than at the time Thatcher had come to power.

In 1999 the new government lowered the first income tax rate from 20 to 10 per cent, but it also reduced the basic allowance. It increased effective rates on middle and higher incomes by abolishing tax reliefs on pensions, mortgages and corporate taxes (OECD, 2002). In later years the govern-ment moderately increased several major taxes and it also benefited from fiscal drag in the wake of the economic boom. The additional revenues were largely used to increase spending in health and education, and to improve the pensions of poor people (OECD, 2004a).

New Labour also enhanced employment policies that improved the job opportunities of young people and families (Rueda, 2006). In particular, it expanded in-work benefits considerably: it replaced the old 'Family Credit' by the 'Working Family Tax Credit' (WFTC), a tax credit granted to poor families with children. Compared with the German Mainzer Modell it is much more generous, since the tax credit is worth some 30 to 35 per cent of the wage of an average production worker (OECD, 2005: 144). It is also more costly in terms of government revenues, totalling some 0.6 per cent of GDP. Although it is designed to improve the compatibility between work and welfare benefits it is obvious that the WFTC has a clear redis-tributive purpose (Dilnot and McCrae, 2000: 79).[16] Given its sheer size it is therefore important to include it in a discussion of the progressivity of the tax system.

All things considered, the Blair government clearly steered away from the idea of shedding jobs with low productivity, but rather focused on welfare-to-work and work-first principles (Glyn and Wood, 2001). Again several reasons have been put forward to explain this shift in political positions of the left. Alt, Preston and Sibieta (2007), for instance, note that during the 1980s and 1990s the median-voter position on tax versus spending issues moved considerably to the right of the political spectrum. Manifesto and expert opinion data (Laver, Benoit and Garry, 2003) shows that Labour accommodated this move. It is nowadays much more centric than some 20 years ago. It even leap-frogged the Liberal Democrats to make them the political party farthest to the left. Political institutions play a crucial role in understanding the differences between the UK and Germany. Whereas in Germany a party such as the Liberal Democrats could have benefited on Labour's move to the political centre, the electoral system in the UK assured that this danger has been much smaller so far.

The weakness of serious contenders on the left and the detrimental confrontation of the trade unions with the Thatcher government, allowed Labour to loosen its close ties to the trade unions. Already in 1993 the Labour Party Congress reduced the political weight of unions (Rueda, 2006: 9) and started to seek different channels of party finance (Fisher, 1997). To be sure, some trade unions – for example those of the public services – are still very influential in the UK but their political weight nowadays mirrors more closely their economic weight. Somewhat paradoxically, the decreased weight of unions has improved the political room to manoeuvre of Labour somewhat, albeit with the price tag that it moved considerably to the right.

CONCLUSIONS

The empirical evidence corroborates the visible, but ambivalent role of the political left in shaping the tax system. It is clear that political and economic restrictions do play a role, but they do not impede progressivity of the tax system. Left labour power in the form of union density is indeed an important means to achieve tax-based redistribution both across countries and in a dynamic perspective.

We also saw that the institutional context shapes unions' and left parties' interest in tax progressivity. Where labour markets are highly regulated, and high levels of unemployment prevail, insidership arises and weakens the tie between left labour and tax progressivity. The cross-country evidence showed that employment protection and bargaining coverage are two institutions that are candidates for rent generation. The relative decline of income tax is due to several factors among which international competition surely plays an important role. But we also saw that the decline in union membership weakened unions' strength and also shaped their preferences against tax progressivity. We also saw cautious evidence for a mutual dependence of the tax mix and unemployment. Shifting towards income taxation is hence not a bad strategy for fighting unemployment in many countries.

The historical case of nineteenth-century Germany showed that our basic intuition of a nexus between left labour and tax progressivity is correct. Unions and Social Democrats indeed fought for the introduction of progressive income taxation. Compared with today, two contextual factors differed crucially in the nineteenth century: first, labour markets were virtually free of any institutions that could drive wedges between workers; second, wages as a tax base were only about to develop some significance. Even at the turn of the century, the political power of unions was still comparatively small, whereas its economic power increased rapidly. To become mass organizations unions accepted more and more low-skilled workers and acted in accordance with their interests. The government had to take these interests into account since taxing the payroll of workers was not yet a serious alternative to indirect and income taxation.

The comparison of Germany and the UK after the Second World War shows that the strategic situation of left labour has changed dramatically. Unions and labour parties nowadays act in a field of a highly regulated labour market that sharpens the conflict of interest within the electorate. The shift towards labour taxation has made this conflict even more severe. As is to be expected the declining power of left labour has had two consequences: it has clearly weakened the case for tax-based redistribution and re-established higher levels of income inequalities. Since the decline in membership has affected more the fringes of the labour market and especially the low-skilled workers, insiders have even more to lose than before. In the UK a clearly conservative government curtailed union power and shifted the tax mix against progressivity. Somewhat paradoxically, this gave 'New Labour' some degrees of freedom to reintroduce progressivity, although only to a limited extent. In Germany, the political institutions have shaped the behaviour of both unions and political parties. Neither the CDU nor the Social Democrats have ever been able to distance themselves from trade unionism. The shift against tax progressivity was therefore not due to a conservative revolution, but due to institutional drift in the absence of a strong political signal to strengthen income taxation.

These two cases may be contrasted with Sweden where strong and encompassing unions have defended the importance of income taxation and tax-based redistribution against the influences of international competition and conservative ideology (Ganghof, 2006). Again, it is the configuration of the welfare state and, especially, the labour market that are the the crucial reasons why politicization of the tax mix has arisen and to what effect.

NOTES

1. For instance, she includes other tax rates in the instruments so we do not really know whether her indicator describes changes in spending preferences or changes in opportunity costs.
2. The OECD (2004a: 145) provides some data for later years. I also used the European Industrial Relations Observatory (various years) and Fulton (2007) for later years. For New Zealand I recurred to Harbridge and Moulder (1993) and Wilkinson *et al.* (2003).
3. I am very grateful to Reimut Zohlnhöfer for making the data available to me.
4. See http://www.ipw.unibe.ch/content/team/klaus_armingeon/comparative_political_data_sets/index_ger.html.
5. See his web appendix at http://www-personal.umich.edu/~franzese/book.data appendices. pdf for further details. The author himself admits that this is a very crude proxy for income inequality, but it is the indicator with by far the largest scope for both years and countries. A priori, I do not expect very much from this indicator. For 1995, for instance, the correlation between Franzese's indicator and factor income inequality measured by the Gini-coefficient (Milanovic, 2000) was around 0.2 for 15 OECD countries.
6. See the webpage of the Centre D'Etudes Prospectives et D'Information Internationales (http://www.cepii.fr/anglaisgraph/bdd/bdd.htm) for further details.
7. The test compares both equations and rejects the null hypothesis that the differences between both systems are not systematic ($\chi^2 = 139.86***$).
8. The 'consensus' estimates are own calculations on basis of Scholliers and Hannes (1989: 232). They are cumulative growth rates indexed to the year 1860 as 100. Hence it is impossible to compare the levels of real wages in Germany and the UK.
9. Strike and membership data stem from Cronin (1984), Boll (1984) and Hohorst *et al.* (1975). Union data is in thousands of union members. Strike data is numbers of strikes per annum. Note that there are breaks in all series, since the original data come from various sources.
10. 'A rational limitation of the principle of progressive taxation is not possible. It will develop further, once legally acknowledged, towards the direction in which lie the ideals of socialism' (own translation).
11. For definitions see Chapter 2.
12. Trades Union Congress (MSS.292), Modern Records Centre, University of Warwick.
13. If anything the Party Manifesto Data of Budge *et al.* (2001) shows convergence on both the welfare and the economic planning dimension between the 1960s and 1980s.
14. There is some debate whether the Social Democrats' veto was primarily due to substantive differences or electoral motives (Ganghof, 2004; Zohlnhöfer, 2006).
15. During that scandal it was revealed that the Agency grossly overstated the number of successfully placed unemployed (Kemmerling and Bruttel, 2006).
16. In this respect it is very much related to the US Earned Income Tax Credit (Eissa and Hoynes, 2005).

6. Conclusion: employment and redistribution are not incompatible

In a nutshell, the basic message of this book is that employment and tax-based redistribution are not incompatible, even in a globalized economy. If there is conflict, it is of political rather than economic nature. I will briefly summarize the main findings before I proceed to policy proposals that aim at re-balancing employment with tax incentives.

ANALYTIC AND EMPIRICAL CONCLUSIONS

The choice of the tax mix is both politically and economically a highly relevant question. Chapter 2 has shown that the tax mix reveals underlying differences in the tax structure about redistribution, insurance and inclusion. For long these structural features have determined the political mobilization in welfare states. After the Second World War the tax mix of income, payroll and indirect taxation has gained political importance since ever-increasing non-wage labour costs put labour markets under serious pressure. Given the strong demand for public welfare, the discussion has shifted from whether to how to tax labour. The aim is then to combine goals of public policy such as redistribution and a good performance of labour markets. In that respect we have seen that countries differ in how far they use income taxes as a source of financing the welfare state. We also have seen a shift away from income taxes in most OECD countries. As explained in Chapter 2 this arguably has led to an overall tax structure with lower degrees of tax progressivity and, at least for poorer workers, less insurance.

Tax-based redistribution and high employment are not incompatible as Chapter 3 has shown. Economic theory, as has become clear, is ambiguous, once we depart from simple neoclassic models for employment and unemployment. I have argued that it suffices to add a redistributive component to the tax and transfer system to find that the total tax burden affects rate of unemployment. In general, it is not the tax burden, but the tax (and transfer) structure that affects the performance of a labour market. A priori, the three major elements of the tax structure – progressivity, the insurance component, and the tax base – can stir offsetting effects in the labour market. If, however, the causes of unemployment are related to problems of insider behaviour or monopolistic bargaining, income taxation and progressivity are better for employment and unemployment than payroll or indirect taxation. I probed this argument in a set of simple regressions and found corroborative evidence for my claim. Payroll and indirect taxes were shown to matter more for aggregate employment and unemployment than income taxes. The effect seems to be concentrated in the low-wage sector. It has also become clear that there is a substantial cross-country and cross-temporal variation in the coefficients. One major problem was, of course, the issue of endogeneity.

Correspondingly, I reversed the causality in Chapters 4 and 5, asking for the political causes of tax progressivity and the (declining) importance of income taxation in the tax mix. Indeed, income taxation has become more difficult in the age of globalized markets which inherently acts in favour of richer people and secular, conservative political parties (for example Acemoglu and Robinson, 2006), but this picture remains markedly incomplete. Much more than international competition, long-term trends in the growth of real wages and the welfare state have changed the underlying political game: the taxation of labour instead of capital. As I have explained in the historical part of Chapter 5, the choice of the tax mix in the late nineteenth century was a question about capital (and consumer) taxation. Real wages were simply too low, and welfare states and union power were still nascent phenomena. A hundred years later, the maturity of welfare states, industrial relations and wages as a tax base have shifted the focus of attention to decisions of the tax mix as a question on labour taxation.

With this change there come political conflicts within the electorate of employees. Since the preferences of the very rich and highly qualified are, by and large, relatively easy to reconstruct I deliberately focused on a conflict of interest between low- and medium-skilled workers. Whether this cleavage exists or poses a problem depends on the structural and institutional configuration of national labour markets. An important example is here the role of trade unions as a crucial, though in some countries informal veto player.

As Chapter 4 has shown, in theoretical terms there is a bifurcation: in countries where unions are strong and include a large and representative part of the low-wage sector, unions will take interests of low-wage workers into consideration. This will affect the tax mix since it is in the interest of low-skilled people to have a strong progressivity in the tax system on the lower end of the wage scale; in countries where unions are smaller and represent more medium- than low-skilled workers, but unions are still powerful enough, their position on progressivity is not clear any more. To the contrary such unions fear wage dumping and wage competition from the low-wage sector, and they fear the effect of tax progressivity on wage negotiations. In either way unions will still agree on top-end tax progressivity, but refuse to make the tax burden more progressive on the lower end of the wage scale.

The quantitative section of Chapter 5 showed that there is some evidence for this bifurcation. Tax progressivity and the importance of income taxes indeed rise with the strength of trade unions, but they also decline with my measure of surplus coverage: in countries where there is a huge gap between bargaining coverage and union density, tax progressivity is markedly lower. This also holds for a dynamic perspective, in which I controlled for strategic interactions of countries in the wake of tax competition.

The qualitative sections of Chapter 5 have revealed some micro-mechanisms of my claim. In the historical part, we have seen that indeed income taxation and tax progression was a demand of the trade unions and social democratic parties in Wilhelmine Germany. We can see that in a context of a (nearly) institution-free labour market and a tax burden whose incidence lies mainly on capital, political preferences on progressivity follow the classic poor-versus-rich distinction. After the Second World War we can see that this link became weaker and weaker. A comparison of Germany and the UK has revealed why this is the case. Underlying changes in the labour market changed the structural composition of trade unions. They represented a more and more selective sample of dependent employees, and their political preferences shifted in accordance with these trends. In both countries unions and their political allies, social-democratic parties, increasingly saw taxation as a means to achieve productivity-led growth. Progressivity at the lower end of the wage scale was incompatible with such a strategy. In the 1980s the experience of both countries started to diverge. Whereas the Thatcher government implemented a reform package that both reduced tax progressivity and union power, German trade unions have remained strong veto players, even for parties not strongly closely related to unionism. This divergence still has relevance: whereas nowadays we see a Labour government that cautiously, though not ambitiously, tries to reintroduce tax progressivity, the German experience is one of stop-and-go reforms, in which a left government implemented strong cuts in progressivity and thereafter has successfully managed to better the income position of poor workers.

NORMATIVE CONCLUSIONS

Figure 6.1 visualizes the normative concern of this book: a trade-off between regressivity and incentives to work. It shows marginal effective tax rates for an unemployed single person receiving unemployment benefits

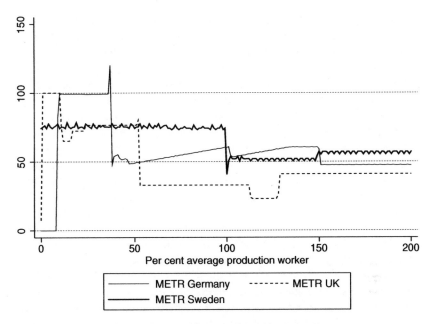

Figure 6.1   Marginal effective tax rates of three countries

at different levels of wage income for the year 2004. I have plotted the
rates for three countries: Germany, Sweden and the UK. One sees that a
full measure of tax progressivity which includes benefit withdrawal rates
reveals regressivity in the tax and benefit system in all countries for wages
below that for the average production worker. In all countries there is a
clear downward jump, once unemployment benefits are faced out. The
jump is highest in Germany, but even in the UK it is considerable and
progressivity does not kick in before a wage level of about 130 per cent.
Compared to this the jump is smaller in Sweden, but nevertheless the marginal rates at twice the wage of an average worker are still lower than for a
worker with half of that wage.

Normative assessments of tax policies and their reforms need a bench-
mark. Many economic analyses use two different forms of normative
standards: Pareto optimality or utilitarian criteria of social welfare. Both
of these normative yardsticks have well-known problems (Rawls, 1971:
Ch. 1.5). On the one hand, Pareto optimality is a very harsh criterion,
which basically rules out most feasible options. It therefore imposes a very
tight status quo bias on the political debate. With heterogeneous people
it is quite unlikely that a reform never hurts anyone in a society. On the
other hand, utilitarian criteria of social welfare all suffer from a similar

problem: They need to make people's utilities in a society comparable so that an optimal social planner can maximize aggregate welfare. This rules out dedication to any specifically sensitive segments of the population, and includes even policy options that are not very desirable from an ethical point of view. Most problematic of all these standards is that they are not impartial and none of it can claim universality.

Therefore, political analyses have to differ from economics in that respect. If politics is seen as the process of how conflicts of interests are settled, then it is very likely that there is a pre-existing dispute over what should be the normative grounds upon which any settlement is to be based. In this case one can only adopt explicitly a partial and ideological position and maximize what is supposed to be the Good under this selective perspective. In recent times, there have been many proposals to relieve this tension in the tax and benefit systems of OECD countries (for an overview see OECD, 2007a). There are several major options at stake, all of which can be roughly related to different political ideologies.

A 'neoliberal' option is to lower the overall tax burden together with a reduction in social benefits. This obviously reduces the jump in the marginal rates and increases unemployed or inactive people's incentives to take up work. This is the typical political package of conservative governments of Reagan or Thatcher (Pierson, 1994). The advantages are the simplicity of such a solution and arguably its effectiveness through material need of poor people. Its major disadvantage is the creation of a low-wage sector which still generates poverty-traps other than work incentives. On empirical terms one sees that both the US and the UK still have considerably larger low-wage sectors than Sweden or Germany (Lucifora *et al.*, 2005).

It is perhaps no coincidence that 'liberal' governments in the US and the UK complemented this strategy with a dramatic increase in targeted subsidies for poor people and their families. In countries where there is a deregulated labour market this will necessarily be more of a redistributive than an employment enhancing tool, but there is also some evidence for mildly positive effects for labour force participation (Blundell and MaCurdy, 1999). In a higher regulated labour market such as Germany the anticipated effects are less obvious. If anything the measures will be very costly or have to be accompanied by drastic cuts in benefit levels as proposed by, for example, Sinn *et al.* (2002).

A different option is to strengthen the ties between contributions and benefits so as to reduce the tax component of social security contributions. This could be a measure in the interest of a conservative reformer caring about the sustainability of the Bismarckian insurance state (Kersbergen, 1995). The reasoning for such a measure is to reestablish the incentives to pay into an insurance, once people perceive the advantages of them

(OECD, 2007a). Given that for poor people insurance schemes will always include a redistributive component, this measure is not very effective for them. But as part of a larger tax package shifting the burden from contributions to direct and indirect taxation it is still a relevant proposal (DIW, 2005; Kenworthy, 2008).

A shift towards income taxation and tax progression is in the interest of an idealized left, social democratic position. Also a shift away from payroll taxes towards VAT may be attractive, but a shift towards more progressivity combines redistributive demands of left voters with work incentives in highly regulated labour markets (see Chapter 3 and Kemmerling, 2005). If this policy option is not available a social democratic perspective could always switch to the inclusion of a degree of progressivity into the system of social security contributions (Scharpf, 1995). In all of these proposals the question remain how to make tax reductions revenue-neutral and how to avoid serious deadweight losses (OECD, 2007a: 173). And yet, there are effective countermeasures at hand such as conditioning tax credits on payroll taxes on an experience basis. If substitutive effects seem threateningly large one may also integrate higher progressivity of the tax system with the regulation of hourly minimum wages or similar measures.

All in all, the discussion makes clear that there is no impartial stance that would reconcile all political aspirations perfectly. Neither is there a 'magic bullet' which would apply to any country (Kenworthy, 2008). It is very likely that labour market institutions complement each other in their effects (Belot and Ours, 2000). In any case, the realization of such proposals depends on the formation of broad political coalitions and the recruitment of strong political allies. This is where a social democratic strategy, or any other political strategy, faces its toughest challenge. For the UK, on the one hand, it remains to be seen whether there is a potential for a welfare state with tax-based redistribution without a strong union movement as a political agent. For Germany, on the other, it rather seems to be how to align union preferences once more behind the idea of tax progressivity and how to compensate unions for concessions they need to make. More than often the deeper roots of economic inefficiencies lie in the political omission of the underprivileged.

Bibliography

Aaberge, R., Dagsvik, J. K. and Strøm, S. (1995), 'Labor supply responses and welfare effects of tax reforms,' *Scandinavian Journal of Economics* **97**(4), 635–59.

Acemoglu, Daron and Robinson, James A. (2006), *Political Origins of Dictatorship and Democracy*, Cambridge, MA: MIT Press.

Adam, Antonis and Kammas, Pantelis (2007), 'Tax policies in a globalized world: Is it politics after all?' *Public Choice* **133**(3–4), 321–41.

Adema, Willem (1999), 'Net social expenditure,' OECD Labour Market and Social Policy – Occasional Papers 38.

Adema, Willem (2001), 'Net social expenditure, 2nd edition,' OECD Labour Market and Social Policy – Occasional Papers 52.

Agell, Jonas (2002), 'On the determinants of labour market institutions: rent seeking vs. social insurance,' *German Economic Review* **3**(2), 107–35.

Alber, Jens (1982), *Vom Armenhaus zum Wohlfahrtsstaat. Analysen zur Entwicklung der Sozialversicherung in Westeuropa*, Frankfurt and New York: Campus.

Alesina, Alberto, Glaeser, Edward and Sacerdote, Bruce (2005), 'Work and leisure in the US and Europe. Why so different?' Harvard Institute of Economic Research Discussion Paper No. 2068.

Alt, James E., Carlsen, Fredrik, Heum, Per and Johansen, Kare (1999), 'Asset specificity and the political behavior of firms: lobbying for subsidies in Norway,' *International Organization* **53**(1), 99–116.

Alt, James, Preston, Ian and Sibieta, Luke (2007), 'The political economy of tax policy,' Mirlees Review Conference.

Atkinson, Anthony B. (1993), 'Work Incentives', in Anthony B. Atkinson and Gunnar V. Mogensen (eds), *Welfare and Work Incentives: A North European Perspective*, Oxford: Clarendon Press, pp. 22–49.

Atkinson, Anthony B. (1995), *Public Economics in Action. The Basic Income/Flat Tax Proposal*, Oxford: Clarendon Press.

Austen-Smith, David (2000), 'Redistributing income under proportional representation,' *Journal of Political Economy* **108**(6), 1235–69.

Baltagi, Badi H. (2005), *Econometric Analysis of Panel Data*, 2nd edn, Chichester *et al.*: Wiley.

Barnhart, Robert K. (1988), *The Barnhart Dictionary of Etymology*, Bronx, NY: H. W. Wilson.

Basinger, Scott and Hallerberg, Mark (2004), 'Remodeling the competition for capital: how domestic politics erases the race to the bottom,' *American Political Science Review* **98**(2), 261–76.

Bawn, Kathleen (1993), 'The logic of institutional preferences – German electoral law as a social choice outcome,' *American Journal of Political Science* **37**(4), 965–89.

Bean, Charles R. (1994), 'European unemployment: a survey,' *Journal of Economic Literature* **32**(2), 573–619.

Beck, Nathaniel and Katz, Jonathan (1996), 'Nuisance vs. substance: specifying and estimating time-series cross-section models,' *Political Analysis* **6**, 1–36.

Bedau, Klaus-Dietrich, Fahrlaender, S., Seidel, B. and Teichmann, D. (1998), 'Wie belastet die Mehrwertsteuererhöhung private Haushalte mit unterschiedlich hohem Einkommen?' *DIW Wochenbericht* 14/98.

Belot, Mich'le and van Ours, Jan (2000), 'Does the recent success of some OECD countries in lowering their unemployment rates lie in the clever design of their labour market reforms?' CEPR Discussion Papers No. 2000-40.

Beramendi, Pablo and Rueda, David (2007), 'Social democracy constrained: indirect taxation in industrialized democracies,' *British Journal of Political Science* **37**(4), 619–41.

Besley, Timothy and Anne Case (1995), 'Incumbent behavior: vote-seeking, tax-setting, and yardstick competition,' *American Economic Review* **85**(1), 25–45.

Blanchard, Olivier J. and Fischer, Stanley (1989), *Lectures on Macroeconomics*, Boston, MA: MIT Press.

Blanchard, Olivier J. and Wolfers, Justin (1999), 'The role of shocks and institutions in the rise of European unemployment: the aggregate evidence,' NBER Working Paper Series 7282.

Bluestone, Barry (2001), A brief primer on inflation theory: the Phillips Curve and NAIRU, in Barry Bluestone and Bennett Harrison (eds), *Growing Prosperity: The Battle for Growth with Equity in the 21st Century*, Berkeley, CA: University of California Press.

Blundell, Richard (1995), 'The impact of taxation on labour force participation and labour supply,' The OECD Jobs Study Working Paper Series 8.

Blundell, Richard and MaCurdy, Thomas (1999), 'Labor supply: a review of alternative approaches', in Orsley Ashenfelter and David Card (eds), *Handbook of Labor Economics* Vol. 3a, North-Holland: Elsevier, pp. 1559–730.

Boeri, Tito, Börsch-Supan, Axel and Tabellini, Guido (2001), 'Would you like to shrink the welfare state? A survey of European citizens,' *Economic Policy* **32**(April), 9–50.

Boix, Carles (1998), *Political Parties, Growth and Equality. Conservative and Social Democratic Economic Strategies in the World Economy*, Cambridge: Cambridge University Press.

Boix, Carles (2003), *Democracy and Redistribution*, Cambridge: Cambridge University Press.

Boll, Friedhelm (1984), Streikwellen im europäischen Vergleich, in Wolfgang C. Mommsen and Hans-Gerhard Husung (eds), *Auf dem Wege zur Massengewerkschaft. Die Entwicklung der Gewerkschaften in Deutschland und Grossbritannien 1880–1914*, Stuttgart: Klett-Cotta, pp. 109–34.

Borck, Rainald (2002), 'Jurisdiction size, political participation, and the allocation of resources,' *Public Choice* 113, 251–63.

Borjas, George J. (2004), *Labor Economics*, 3rd edn, Boston, MA: McGraw-Hill.

Brawley, Mark R. (1997), 'Factoral or sectoral conflict? Partially mobile factors and the politics of trade in imperial Germany,' *International Studies Quarterly* 41(4), 633–53.

Brewer, Mike, Goodman, Alissa, Muriel, Alistair and Sibieta, Luke (2007), Poverty and inequality in the UK: 2007, IFS Briefing Note No. 73. Technical report The Institute for Fiscal Studies.

Brey, Gerhard (1960), *Wages in Germany 1871–1945*, Ann Arbor, MI: University Microfilms.

Brueckner, Jan K. (2003), 'Strategic interaction among governments: an overview of empirical studies,' *International Regional Science Review* 26(2), 175–88.

Budge, Ian, Klingemann, Hans-Dieter, Volkens, Andrea, Bara, Judith and Tanebaum, Eric (2001), *Mapping Policy Preferences – Estimates for Parties, Electors, and Governments 1945–1998*, Oxford: Oxford University Press.

Bundestag, Deutscher (2006), Unterrichtung durch die Bundesregierung: Bericht 2006 der Bundesregierung zur Wirksamkeit moderner Dienstleistungen am Arbeitsmarkt. Technical report Bundestag.

Calmfors, Lars and Driffill, J. (1988), 'Bargaining structure, corporatism and macroeconomic performance,' *Economic Policy* 6, 12–61.

Carey, David and Rabensona, Josette (2002), 'Tax ratios on labour and capital income and on consumption,' *OECD Economic Studies* 35, 130–74.

Carruth, Alan and Schnabel, Claus (1990), 'Empirical modelling of trade union growth in Germany, 1956–1986: traditional versus cointegration and error correction methods,' *Review of World Economics* 126(2), 326–46.

Castles, Francis G. (2004), 'Developing new measures of welfare state change and reform,' *European Journal of Political Research* 41, 613–41.

Chang, Juin-jen, Lin, Chung-cheng and Lai, Ching-chong (1999), 'The unemployment and wage effects of shifting to an indirect tax in an efficiency wage model,' *Economic Record* **75**(229), 156–66.

Checchi, Daniele and Lucifora, Claudio (2002), 'Unions and labour market institutions in Europe,' *Economic Policy* **35**(October), 363–408.

Chernick, Howard (2005), 'On the determinants of subnational progressivity in the US,' *National Tax Journal* **58**(1), 93–112.

Clark, Andrew E. (2003), 'Looking for labour market rents with subjective data,' CNRS and Delta Working Paper September.

Clark, Gregory (2005), 'The condition of the working class in England, 1209–2004,' *Journal of Political Economy* **113**(6), 1307–40.

Corneo, Giacomo (2005), 'The rise and likely fall of the German income tax, 1958–2005,' *CESifo Economic Studies* **51**(1), 159–86.

Cox, Robert Henry (2001), 'The social construction of an imperative. Why welfare reform happened in Denmark and the Netherlands but not in Germany,' *World Politics* **53**(April), 463–98.

Cronin, James E. (1984), 'Streiks und gewerkschaftliche Organisationsfortschritte. Grossbritannien und Kontinentaleuropa 1870–1914', in Wolfgang C. Mommsen and Hans-Gerhard Husung (eds), *Auf dem Wege zur Massengewerkschaft. Die Entwicklung der Gewerkschaften in Deutschland und Grossbritannien 1880–1914*, Stuttgart: Klett-Cotta, pp. 79–108.

Cusack, Thomas R. and Beramendi, Pablo (2006), 'Taxing work: some political and economic aspects of labor income taxation,' *European Journal of Political Research* **45**(1), 43–73.

Daunton, Martin (2002), *Just Taxes. The Politics of Taxation in Britain, 1914–1979*, Cambridge: Cambridge University Press.

Daveri, Francesco (2001), Labor taxes and unemployment: A survey of the aggregate evidence, in *2nd Annual CERP Conference on Pension Policy Harmonization in an Integrating Europe*, 22–23 June, Moncalieri, Turin: Mimeograph.

Daveri, Franceso and Guido Tabellini (2000), 'Unemployment, growth and taxation in industrial countries,' *Economic Policy* **30**(April), 48–104.

Dehejia, Vivek H. and Genschel, Philipp (1998), 'Tax competition in the European Union,' MPIfG Discussion Paper 98/3.

Desai, Ashok V. (1968), *Real Wages in Germany 1871–1913*, Oxford: Oxford Clarendon Press.

Devereux, Michael P., Griffith, Rachel and Klemm, Alexander (2002), 'Corporate income tax reforms and international tax competition,' *Economic Policy* **17**, 451–95.

Dilnot, Andrew and McCrae, Julian (2000), 'The family credit system and the working families tax credit in the United Kingdom,' *OECD Economic Studies* **31**(2000/II).

Disney, Richard (2000), 'The impact of tax and welfare policies on employment and unemployment in OECD countries,' IMF Working Paper WP/00/164.

Disney, Richard (2004), 'Pensions and employment. Are contributions to public pension programmes a tax on employment?' *Economic Policy* (July), 267–311.

DIW (2005), 'Gesamtwirtschaftliche Wirkungen einer Steuerfinanzierung versicherungsfremder Leistungen in der Sozialversicherung,' DIW Berlin: Politikberatung kompakt März.

Ebbinghaus, Bernhard (2002), *Exit from Labour. Reforming Early Retirement and Social Partnership in Europe, Japan, and the USA.* Habilitationsschrift Universität Köln: Mimeograph.

Ebbinghaus, Bernhard and Visser, Jelle (2000), *Trade Unions in Western Europe since 1945*, London: Macmillan.

Edlund, Jonas and Aberg, Rune (2002), 'Social norms and tax compliance,' *A Swedish Economic Policy Review* **9**, 201–28.

Egle, Christoph and Zohlnhöfer, Reimut (2007), 'Projekt oder Episode was bleibt von Rot-Grün', in Christoph Egle and Reimut Zohlnhöfer (eds), *Ende des rot-grünen Projekts. Eine Bilanz der Regierung Schröder 2002–2005*, Wiesbaden: VS Verlag, pp. 511–36.

Eissa, Nada O. and Hoynes, Hilary W. (2005), 'Behavioral responses to taxes: lessons from the EITC and labor supply,' NBER Working Paper No. W11729.

Esping-Andersen, Gøsta (1990), *The Three Worlds of Welfare Capitalism*, Cambridge: Polity Press.

Esping-Andersen, Gøsta (1999), *Social Foundations of Postindustrial Economies*, Oxford: Oxford University Press.

Estevez-Abe, Margarita, Iversen, Torben and Soskice, David (2001), 'Social protection and the formation of skills: a reinterpretation of the welfare state', in Peter Hall and David Soskice (eds), *Varieties of Capitalism: The Institutional Foundations of Comparative Advantage*, Oxford: Oxford University Press, pp. 145–83.

Eurostat (2004), *Structures of the taxation systems in the European Union. Report – theme 2 economy and finance*, EU: Eurostat.

Eurostat (2004), 'Structures of the taxation systems in the European Union', Eurostat Report – Theme 2, Economy and Finance, Brussels.

Fisher, Justin (1997), 'Donations to political parties,' *Parliamentary Affairs* **50**(2), 235–45.

Fogel, Robert (1990), 'The conquest of high mortality and hunger in Europe and America: timing and mechanisms,' NBER Historical Working Paper 0016.

Franz, Wolfgang (1993), *Arbeitsmarktökonomik*, Berlin: Springer.

Franzese, Robert J. (2002), *Macroeconomic Policies of Developed Democracies*, Cambridge: Cambridge University Press.

Franzese, Robert J. and Hays, Jude (2004), 'Empirical modeling strategies for spatial interdependence: omitted-variable vs. simultaneity bias,' Mimeograph 24 July.

Franzese, Robert and Hays, Jude (2007), 'Empirical models of international capital-tax competition', in G. Gregoriou and C. Read (eds), *International Taxation Handbook*, Amsterdam: Elsevier, pp. 44–72.

Fuest, Clemens (2000), *Steuerpolitik und Arbeitslosigkeit*, Tübingen: Mohr Siebeck.

Fulton, L. (2007), 'Worker representation in Europe. Labour Research Department and ETUI-REHS: 2007,' Labour Research Department and ETUIREHS http://www.worker-participation.eu/.

Ganghof, Steffen (2000), 'Adjusting national tax policy to economic internationalization. strategies and outcomes', in Fritz W. Scharpf and Vivien A. Schmidt (eds), *Welfare and Work in the Open Economy, Vol. II: Diverse Responses to Common Challenges*, Oxford: Oxford University Press, pp. 597–645.

Ganghof, Steffen (2004), *Wer regiert in der Steuerpolitik? Einkommensteuerreform zwischen internationalem Wettbewerb und nationalen Verteilungskonflikten*, Frankfurt a.M. and New York: Campus.

Ganghof, Steffen (2006), *The Politics of Income Taxation. A Comparative Analysis*, Political Science Colchester: ECPR Press.

Garrett, Geoffrey (1998), *Partisan Politics in the Global Economy*, Cambridge: Cambridge University Press.

Geddes, Barbara (2003), *Paradigms and Sand Castles. Theory Building and Research Design in Comparative Politics*, Ann Arbor, MI: University of Michigan Press.

Genschel, Philipp (2002), 'Globalization, tax competition, and the welfare state,' *Politics & Society* **30**(2), 245–75.

Glyn, Andrew and Wood, Stewart (2001), 'Economic policy under New Labour: how social democratic is the Blair Government?' *The Political Quarterly* **72**(1), 50–66.

Goerke, Laszlo (2002), *Taxes and Unemployment*, Boston, MA, Dordrecht and London: Kluwer Academic Publishers.

Gould, Andrew C. and Baker, Peter J., (2002), 'Democracy and taxation,' *Annual Review of Political Science* **5**, 87–110.

Greskovits, Bela (1998), *The Political Economy of Protest and Patience. East European and Latin American Transformations Compared*, Budapest: Central European University Press.

Gustafsson, Siv (1996), 'Tax regimes and labour market performance', in Günther Schmid, Jaqueline O'Reilly and Klaus Schoemann (eds), International Handbook of Labour Market Policy and Evaluation, Cheltenham: Edward Elgar, pp. 811–39.

Haan, Jakob de, Sturm, Jan-Egbert and Volkerink, Bjørn (2003), 'How to measure the tax burden on labour at the macro-level?' CESifo Working Paper No. 963.

Hallerberg, Mark (1996), 'Tax competition in Wilhelmine Germany and its implications for the European Union,' *World Politics* **48**(3), 324–57.

Hallerberg, Mark and Basinger, Scott (1998), 'Internationalization and changes in tax policy in OECD countries. The importance of domestic veto players,' *Comparative Political Studies* **31**(3), 321–52.

Hamermesh, Daniel S. (1993), *Labor Demand*. Princeton, NJ: Princeton University Press.

Hansen, Claus T., Pedersen, Lars H. and Slok, Torsten (2000), 'Ambiguous effects of tax progressivity – theory and Danish evidence,' *Labour Economics* **7**(3), 335–47.

Harbridge, Raymond and Moulder, James (1993), 'Collective bargaining and New Zealand's employment contracts act: one year on,' *Journal of Industrial Relations* **35**(1), 62–83.

Hartlapp, Miriam and Kemmerling, Achim (2008), 'When a solution becomes the problem: The causes for policy reversal of early exit from the labour force,' *Journal of European Social Policy* **18**(4), 366–79.

Haucap, Justus, Pauly, Uwe and Wey, Christian (1999), 'The incentives of employers associations to raise rivals costs in the presence of collective bargaining,' WZB discussion papers FS IV 99-6.

Hays, Jude (2003), 'Globalization and capital taxation in consensus and majoritarian democracies,' *World Politics* **56**, 79–113.

Heady, Christopher (2004), 'The "Taxing wages" approach to measuring the tax burden on labour', in Peter Birch Sørensen (ed.), *Measuring Taxes on Capital and Labor*, CESIfo Seminar Series, Cambridge, MA and London: MIT Press, pp. 263–87.

Heijdra, Ben J. and van der Ploeg, Frederick (2002), *Foundations of Modern Macroeconomics*, Oxford: Oxford University Press.

Heinze, Rolf G. and Streeck, Wolfgang (2003), 'Optionen für den Einstieg in den Arbeitsmarkt oder: Ein Lehrstück für einen gescheiterten Politikwechsel,' *Vierteljahreshefte zur Wirtschaftsforschung* **72**(1), 25–35.

Henning, Friedrich-Wilhelm (1996), *Handbuch der Wirtschafts- und Sozialgeschichte Deutschlands*. Vol. 2, Paderborn: Ferdinand Schöningh.

Hettich, Walter and Winer, Stanley L. (1999), *Democratic Choice and Taxation. A Theoretical and Empirical Analysis*, Cambridge: Cambridge University Press.

Hindriks, Jean (2001), 'Is there a demand for income tax progressivity?' *Economic Letters* **73**, 43–50.

Hinich, Melvin J. and Munger, Michael C. (1997), *Analytical Politics*, Cambridge: Cambridge University Press.

Hohorst, Gerd, Kocka, Juergen and Ritter, Gerhard (1975), *Sozialgeschichtliches Arbeitsbuch. Materialien zur Statistik des Kaiserreichs 1870–1914*, Muenchen: Beck.

Homburg, Stefan (2003), *Allgemeine Steuerlehre*, 2nd edn, München: Verlag Wahlen.

Howard, Christopher (1997), *The Hidden Welfare State: Tax Expenditures and Social Policy in the United States. Princeton Studies in American Politics*, Princeton, NJ: Princeton University Press.

Hutton, John P. and Ruocco, Anna (1999), 'Tax reform and employment in Europe,' *International Tax and Public Finance* **6**(3), 263–87.

Immergut, Ellen M. (1992), *Health Politics: Interests and Institutions in Western Europe*, Cambridge: Cambridge University Press.

Iversen, Torben (1999), *Contested Economic Institutions*, Cambridge: Cambridge University Press.

Iversen, Torben (2000), 'Decentralization, monetarism, and the social democratic welfare state', in Torben Iversen, Jonas Pontusson and David Soskice (eds), *Unions, Employers, and Central Banks*, Cambridge: Cambridge University Press, pp. 1–37.

Iversen, Torben and Cusack, Thomas R. (2000), 'The causes of welfare state expansion: deindustrialization or globalization?' *World Politics* **52**, 313–49.

Iversen, Torben and Soskice, David (2001), 'An asset theory of social policy preferences,' *American Political Science Review* **95**(4), 875–93.

Johnson, Paul and Webb, Steven (1993), 'Explaining the growth in UK income inequality: 1979–1988,' *The Economic Journal* **103**(417), 429–35.

Kanbur, Ravi and Keen, Michael (2001), 'Jeux sans frontières: tax competition and tax coordination when countries differ in size,' *American Economic Review*, **September**, 877–92.

Kato, Junko (2003), *Regressive Taxation and the Welfare State. Path Dependence and Policy Diffusion*, Cambridge: Cambridge University Press.

Kemmerling, Achim (2003), 'Die Rolle des Wohlfahrtsstaates in der Entwicklung unterschiedlicher Dienstleistungssektoren,' WZB discussion papers SP I 2003-108.

Kemmerling, Achim (2004), Die Messung sozialstaatlicher Leistungen Brutto- und Nettosozialleistungsquote, in Statistisches Bundesamt, *Ökonomische Leistungsfähigkeit Deutschlands. Bestandsaufnahme und statistische Messung im internationalen Vergleich*, Wiesbaden: Statistisches Bundesamt, pp. 150–72.

Kemmerling, Achim (2005), 'Tax mixes, welfare states and employment: tracking diverging vulnerabilities,' *Journal of European Public Policy* **12**(1), 1–22.

Kemmerling, Achim (2006), 'Redistribution or regulation? The political economy of taxing the low-wage sector,' Annual meeting of the American Political Science Association (Marriott, Loews Philadelphia, and the Pennsylvania Convention Center, Philadelphia).

Kemmerling, Achim (2007), 'The end of work or work without end? The role of voters' beliefs in shaping policies of early exit,' WZB discussion papers SP I 2007, 108.

Kemmerling, Achim and Bruttel, Oliver (2006), '"New politics" in German labour market policy? The implications of the recent Hartz reforms for the German welfare state,' *West European Politics* **29**(1), 90–112.

Kenworthy, Lane (2001), 'Wage-setting measures. A survey and assessment,' *World Politics* **54**(October), 57–98.

Kenworthy, L. (2003), 'Do affluent countries face an incomes-jobs trade-off?' *Comparative Political Studies* **36**(10), 1180–209.

Kenworthy, Lane (2008), *Jobs with Equality*, Oxford: Oxford University Press.

Kersbergen, Kees van (1995), *Social Capitalism. A Study of Christian Democracy and the Welfare State*, London and New York: Routledge.

Kim, Hee-Min and Fording, Richard C. (2001), 'Extending party estimates to governments and electors', in Ian Budge, HansDieter Klingemann, Andrea Volkens, Judith Bara and Eric Tanebaum (eds), *Mapping Policy Preferences – Estimates for Parties, Electors, and Governments 1945–1998*, Oxford: Oxford University Press, pp. 157–79.

Kitschelt, Herbert (1994), *The Transformation of European Social Democracy*, Cambridge: Cambridge University Press.

Kittel, Bernhard (2001), 'How bargaining mediates wage determination: an exploration of the parameters of wage functions in a pooled time-series cross-section framework,' MPIfG Discussion Paper 01/ 3.

Kittel, Bernhard (2003), Politische Ökonomie der Arbeitsbeziehungen, in Bernhard Kittel, Herbert Obinger and Uwe Wagschal (eds), *Politische Ökonomie*, Opladen: Leske und Budrich, pp. 81–109.

Kittel, Bernhard and Obinger, Herbert (2003), 'Political parties, institutions, and the dynamics of social expenditure in times of austerity,' *Journal of European Public Policy* **10**(1), 20–45.

Kittel, Bernhard and Winner, Hannes (2005), 'How reliable is pooled analysis in political economy? The globalization-welfare state nexus revisited,' *European Journal of Political Research* **44**(2), 269–94.

Kok, Wim (2003), Jobs, Jobs, Jobs. Creating more employment in Europe. Report of the Employment Taskforce, Technical report European Union.

Korpi, Walter and Palme, Joakim (1998), 'The paradox of redistribution and strategies of equality: welfare state institutions, inequality, and poverty in the Western Countries,' *American Sociological Review* **63**(October), 661–87.

Koskela, Erkki and Holm, Pasi (1995), 'Tax progression, structure of labour taxation and employment,' CESifo Working Paper No. 91.

Krugman, Paul R. and Obstfeld, Maurice (1997), *International Economics. Theory and Policy*, Reading, MA: Addison-Wesley.

Laisney, Francois, Pohlmeier, Winfried and Staat, Matthias (1995), 'Estimation of labour supply functions using panel data: a survey', in Laszlo Matyas and Patrick Sevestre (eds), *The Econometrics of Panel Data. A Handbook of the Theory with Applications*, Dordrecht, Boston, MA and London: Kluwer, pp. 733–70.

Laver, Michael, Benoit, Kenneth and Garry, John (2003), 'Extracting policy positions from political texts using words as data,' *American Political Science Review* **97**(02), 311–31.

Layard, Richard, Nickell, Stephen and Jackman, Richard (1991), *Unemployment. Macroeconomic Performance and the Labour Market*, Oxford: Oxford University Press.

Lazear, Edward (1990), 'Job security provisions and employment,' *The Quarterly Journal of Economics* **105**(3), 699–726.

Lee, Woojin and Roemer, John E. (2005), 'The rise and fall of unionised labour markets: a political economy approach,' *The Economic Journal* **115**(500), 28–67.

Levy, Jonah (2000), 'Directing adjustment? The politics of welfare reform in France', in Fritz W. Scharpf and Vivien A. Schmidt (eds), *Welfare and Work in the Open Economy*, Vol. I, Oxford: Oxford University Press, pp. 19–68.

Lijphart, Arend (1994), *Electoral Systems and Party Systems*, Oxford: Oxford University Press.

Lindbeck, A. (1995), 'Welfare state disincentives with endogenous habits and norms,' *Scandinavian Journal of Economics* **97**(4), 477–94.

Lindbeck, Assar and Snower, Dennis (1986), 'Wage setting, unemployment and insider-outsider relations,' *American Economic Review* **76**(2), 235–9.

Lindert, Peter (2004), *Growing Public: Social Spending and Economic Growth since the Eighteenth Century*, Vol. 1, Cambridge: Cambridge University Press.

Lockwood, Ben and Manning, Alan (1993), 'Wage setting and the tax-system – theory and evidence for the United Kingdom,' *Journal of Public Economics* **52**(1), 1–29.

Lucifora, Claudio, McKnight, Abigail and Salverda, Weimer (2005), 'Low-wage employment in Europe: a review of the evidence,' *Socio-Economic Review* **3**, 259–92.

Manow, Philip (2002), "The good, the bad and the ugly". Esping Andersens Sozialstaats-Typologie und die konfessionellen Wurzeln des westlichen Wohlfahrtsstaates,' *Kölner Zeitschrift für Soziologie und Sozialpsychologie* **54**(2), 203–25.

Manow, Philip and Seils, Eric (2000), 'The employment crisis of the German welfare state,' *West European Politics* **23**(2), 138–60.

Mares, Isabela (2006), *Taxation, Wage Bargaining and Unemployment*, Cambridge: Cambridge University Press.

Marx, Karl (1989 [1848]), *Manifest der kommunistischen Partei*, 16th edn, Berlin (London): Dietz.

Mattli, Walter (1999), *The Logic of Regional Integration. Europe and Beyond*, Cambridge: Cambridge University Press.

McKenzie, Baker & (1999), *Survey of the Effective Tax Burden in the European Union*, Technical report.

Meidner, Rudolf and Hedborg, Anna (1984), *Modell Schweden. Erfahrungen einer Wohlstandsgesellschaft*, Köln: Bund-Verlag.

Meltzer, Allan and Richard, Scott F. (1991), 'A Rational Theory of the Size of Government', in Allan Meltzer, Alex Cukierman and Scott F. Richard (eds), *Political Economy*, Oxford: Oxford University Press, pp. 23–35.

Mendoza, Enrique G., Razin, Assaf and Tesar, Linda L. (1994), 'Effective tax rates in macroeconomics: Cross-country estimates of tax rates on factor incomes and consumption,' *Journal of Monetary Economics* **34**, 297–323.

Messere, Ken C. (1993), *Tax Policy in OECD Countries: Choices and Conflicts*, Amsterdam: IBFD Publications.

Milanovic, Branko (2000), 'The median voter hypothesis, income inequality and income redistribution: An empirical test with the required data,' *European Journal of Political Economy* **16**, 367–410.

Milyo, Jeffrey (2000), 'Logical deficiencies in spatial models: A constructive critique,' *Public Choice* **105**, 273–89.

Moene, Karl Ove and Wallerstein, Michael (2001), 'Inequality, social insurance, and redistribution,' *American Political Science Review* **95**(4), 859–74.

Montanari, Ingalill (2001), 'Modernization, globalization and the welfare state: a comparative analysis of old and new convergence of social insurance since 1930,' *British Journal of Sociology* **52**(3), 469–94.

Mueller, Dennis (2003), *Public Choice III*, Cambridge: Cambridge University Press.

Nickell, Stephen (1997), 'Unemployment and labor market rigidities: Europe versus North America,' *Journal of Economic Perspectives* **11**, 55–74.

Nickell, Stephen and Layard, Richard (1999), 'Labor market institutions and economic performance', in Orley Ashenfelter and David Card (eds), *Handbook of Labor Economics*, Vol. 3c, Amsterdam: Elsevier, pp. 3029–83.

O'Brien, Patrick K. (1988), 'The political economy of British taxation, 1660–1815,' *Economic History Review* **41**(1), 1–32.

Ochel, Wolfgang (2001), 'Collective bargaining coverage in the OECD from the 1960s to the 1990s,' *CESIfo Forum* **2**(4), 62–5.

OECD (1990), 'Employer versus employee taxation: the impact on employment,' *Employment Outlook 1990*: 153–76.

OECD (1995), *Taxation, Employment and Unemployment*, The OECD Jobs Study, Paris: OECD Publications.

OECD (1996), 'Earnings inequality, low-paid employment and earnings mobility,' *OECD Employment Outlook 1996*, 59–107.

OECD (1997a), 'Economic performance and the structure of collective bargaining,' *OECD Economic Outlook 1997*, 63–92.

OECD (1997b), *Making Work Pay: Taxation, Benefits, Employment and Unemployment*, The OECD Jobs Strategy, Paris: OECD Publishing.

OECD (1998), 'Revenue statistics 1965–1997,' *Revenue Statistics Edition 1998*.

OECD (1999a), 'Employment protection and labour market performance', in OECD (ed.), *OECD Employment Outlook 1999*, Paris: OECD, pp. 48–130.

OECD (1999b), 'Tax revenue trends, 1965–1998,' *Revenue Statistics 1965–1998*, 17–39.

OECD (2002), *Economic Survey: United Kingdom*, Technical report OECD.

OECD (2004a), *Economic Survey: United Kingdom*, Technical report OECD.

OECD (2004b), *Taxing Wages 2003/2004*, Technical report OECD.

OECD (2005), *OECD Employment Outlook 2005*, Paris: OECD.

OECD (2007a), *OECD Employment Outlook 2007*, Paris: OECD.

OECD (2007b), *Tax Administration in OECD and Selected Non-OECD Countries: Comparative Information Series (2006)*, Paris: OECD.

Olson, Mancur (1965), *The Logic of Collective Action*, Cambridge, MA: Harvard University Press.

Oswald, Andrew J. (1982), 'The microeconomic theory of the trade union,' *Economic Journal* **92**(367), 576–95.

Oswald, Andrew J. (1993), 'Efficient contracts are on the labour demand curve: Theory and facts,' *Labour Economics* **1**(1), 85–113.

Palokangas, Tapio (2003), 'The political economy of collective bargaining,' *Labour Economics* **10**(2), 253–64.

Persson, Torsten and Tabellini, Guido (2002), *Political Economics. Explaining Economic Policy*, Cambridge, MA and London: MIT Press.

Persson, Torsten and Tabellini, Guido (2003), *The Economic Effects of Constitutions*, Cambridge, MA and London: MIT Press.

Pfeifer, Wolfgang *et al.* (1993), *Etymologisches Wörterbuch des Deutschen*, Vol. Band 2, Berlin: Akademie Verlag.

Pierson, P. (1994), *Dismantling the Welfare State? Reagan, Thatcher, and the Politics of Retrenchment*, Cambridge: Cambridge University Press.

Pierson, P. (1996), 'The new politics of the welfare state,' *World Politics* **48**(2), 143–79.

Pierson, P. (2004), *Politics in Time. History, Institutions, and Social Analysis*, Princeton, NJ: Princeton University Press.

Pinto-Duschinsky, Michael (1989), 'Trends in British party funding 1983–1987,' *Parliamentary Affairs* **42**(April), 197–212.

Pissarides, Christopher A. (1992), 'Loss of skill during unemployment and the persistence of employment shocks,' *Quarterly Journal of Economics* **107**, 1371–91.

Pissarides, Christopher A. (1998), 'The impact of employment tax cuts on unemployment and wages. The role of unemployment benefits and tax structure,' *European Economic Review* **42**, 155–83.

Przeworski, Adam and Wallerstein, Michael (1988), 'Structural dependence of the state on capital,' *American Political Science Review* **82**(1), 11–29.

Quinn, Dennis (1997), 'The correlates of change in international financial regulation,' *American Political Science Review* **91**(3), 531–50.

Rawls, John (1971), *A Theory of Justice*, Cambridge, MA: Harvard University Press.

Rehm, Philipp (2005), 'Citizen support for the welfare state: determinants of preferences for income redistribution,' *WZB discussion papers SP II 2005-02*.

Rhodes, Martin (2000), 'Restructuring the British welfare state: between domestic constraints and global imperatives', in Fritz W. Scharpf and

Vivien A. Schmidt (eds), *Welfare and Work in the Open Economy*, Vol. II, Oxford: Oxford University Press, pp. 19–68.

Riley, Nicola-Maria (1997), 'Determinants of union membership: a review,' *Labour* **11**(2), 265–301.

Ritter, Gerhard (1963), *Die Arbeiterbewegung im Wilhelminischen Kaiserreich. Die sozialdemokratische Partei und die freien Gewerkschaften 1890–1990*, Berlin: Colloquium Verlag.

Ritter, Gerhard (1997), 'Sozialpolitik im Zeitalter Bismarcks. Ein Bericht ber neue Quelleneditionen und neue Literatur,' *Historische Zeitschrift* **265**, 683–720.

Roemer, John E. (1999), 'The democratic political economy of progressive income taxation,' *Econometrica*, **67**(1), 1–19.

Roemer, John E. (2001), *Political Competition. Theory and Applications*, Cambridge, MA, London: Harvard University Press.

Rudolph, Helmut (2003), 'Mini- und Midi-Jobs. Geringfügige Beschäftigung im neuen Outfit,' *IAB Kurzbericht*, **6**(23.5.2003).

Rueda, David (2005), 'Insider–outsider politics in industrialized democracies: the challenge to social democratic parties,' *American Political Science Review*, **99**(1), 61–74.

Rueda, David (2006), 'Social democracy and active labour-market policies: insiders, outsiders and the politics of employment promotion,' *British Journal of Political Science* **36**(3), 385–406.

Sachverständigenrat zur Begutachtung der gesamtwirtschaftlichen Entwicklung, SVR. (2003), Staatsfinanzen konsolidieren – Steuersystem reformieren. Jahresgutachten 2003/2004, Technical report SVR.

Saint-Paul, Gilles (2000), *The Political Economy of Labour Market Institutions*, Oxford: Oxford University Press.

Saint-Paul, Gilles (2004), 'Why are European countries diverging in their unemployment experience?' *Journal of Economic Perspectives* **18**(4), 49–68.

Sanandaji, Tino and Wallace, Björn (2003), '*Fiscal Illusion and Fiscal Obfuscation: An Empirical Study of Tax Perception in Sweden,*' Stockholm: Stockholm School of Economics.

Satz, Debra and Ferejohn, John (1994), 'Rational choice and social theory,' *The Journal of Philosophy* **91**(2), 71–87.

Scharpf, Fritz W. (1987), *Sozialdemokratische Krisenpolitik in Europa*, 2nd edn, Frankfurt a.M.: Campus.

Scharpf, Fritz W. (1995), 'Subventionierte Niedriglohn-Beschäftigung statt bezahlter Arbeitslosigkeit?' *Zeitschrift für Sozialreform* **41**(2), 65–83.

Scharpf, Fritz W. (1999), *Regieren in Europa: effektiv und demokratisch?* Frankfurt a.M. and New York: Campus.

Scharpf, Fritz W. (2000), 'Economic changes, vulnerabilities, and institutional capabilities', in Fritz W. Scharpf and Vivien A. Schmidt (eds), *Welfare and Work in the Open Economy*, Vol. I, *From Vulnerability to Competitiveness*, Oxford: Oxford University Press, pp. 21–124.

Schmid, Günther (2006), 'Der kurze Traum der Vollbesch"ftigung: Was lehren 55 Jahre deutsche Arbeitsmarkt- und Besch"ftigungspolitik?' in Manfred G. Schmidt and Reimut Zohlnhöfer (eds), *Regieren in der Bundesrepublik Deutschland. Innen- und Aussenpolitik seit 1949*, Wiesbaden: VS Verlag für Sozialwissenschaften, pp. 177–201.

Schmid, Günther, Reissert, Bernd and Bruche, Gert (1987), *Arbeitslosenversicherung und aktive Arbeitsmarktpolitik. Finanzierungssysteme im internationalen Vergleich*, Berlin: Edition Sigma.

Schmidt, Manfred G. (1982), *Wohlfahrtsstaatliche Politik unter bürgerlichen und sozial-demokratischen Regierungen. Ein Internationaler Vergleich*, Frankfurt a.M.: Campus.

Schmidt, Manfred G. (1998), *Sozialpolitik in Deutschland: Historische Entwicklung und internationaler Vergleich*, 2nd edn, Opladen: Leske + Budrich.

Schmidt, Vivien A. (2000), 'Values and discourse in the politics of adjustment', In Fritz W. Scharpf and Vivien A. Schmidt (eds), *Welfare and Work in the Open Economy*, Vol. I, Oxford: Oxford University Press, pp. 229–310.

Schnabel, Claus (2003), 'Determinants of union membership', in John T. Addison and Claus Schnabel (eds), *International Handbook of Trade Unions*, Cheltenham: Edward Elgar, pp. 13–44.

Schneider, Friedrich (2002), 'Zunehmende Schattenwirtschaft in Deutschland: eine wirtschafts- und staatspolitische Herausforderung,' *Vierteljahreshefte des DIW – Sondernummer Niedriglohnsektor in Deutschland Herbst 2002*, http://www.econ.jku.at/members/Schneider/files/publications/DIW.PDF.

Schneider, Kerstin (2004), 'Union wage setting and progressive income taxation with heterogeneous labor: theory and evidence from the German income tax reforms 1986–1990,' *Labour Economics* **12**(2), 204–22.

Scholliers, Peter and J. Hannes (1989), 'Some conclusions and suggestions for further research', in Peter Scholliers (ed.), *Real Wages in 19th and 20th Century Europe*, New York, Oxford, Munich: Berg, pp. 229–335.

Schröder, Gerhard and Blair, Tony (1999), 'Der Weg nach vorne für Europas Sozialdemokraten,' Berlin: GLASNOST, http://www.glasnost.de/pol/shroederblair.html

Schwartz, Hermann (2000), 'Internationalization and two liberal welfare states Australia and New Zealand', in Fritz W. Scharpf and Vivien A.

Schmidt (eds), *Welfare and Work in the Open Economy*, Vol. II, Oxford: Oxford University Press, pp. 69–130.

Schwarz, Peter (2007), 'Does capital mobility reduce the corporate-labor tax ratio?' *Public Choice* **130**(3–4), 363–80.

Seebold, Elmar (ed.) (2002), *Etymologisches Wörterbuch der deutschen Sprache*, 24th edn, Berlin and New York: de Gruyter.

Shapiro, Carl and Stiglitz, Joseph E. (1984), 'Equilibrium unemployment as a worker discipline device,' *American Economic Review* **74**(June), 433–44.

Sinn, Gerlinde and Sinn, Hans-Werner (1992), *Jumpstart: the Economic Unification of Germany*, Cambridge, MA: MIT Press.

Sinn, Hans-Werner (1995), 'A theory of the welfare state,' *Scandinavian Journal of Economics* **97**(4), 495–526.

Sinn, Hans-Werner, Holzner, Christian, Meister, Wolfgang, Ochel, Wolfgang and Werding, Martin (2002), 'Aktivierende sozialhilfe. Ein Weg zu mehr Beschäftigung und Wachstum,' *Ifo Schnelldienst*, May, **9**, 3–52.

Smith, Timothy B. (2000), 'The ideology of charity, the image of the English poor law, and debates over the right to assistance in France, 1830–1905,' *The Historical Journal* **40**(04), 997–1032.

Sørensen, Peter Birch (1999), 'Optimal tax progressivity in imperfect labour markets,' *Labour Economics* **6**, 435–52.

Sørensen, Peter Birch (2004), 'Measuring taxes on capital and labor. An overview of methods and issues', in Peter Birch Sorensen (ed.), *Measuring Taxes on Capital and Labor*, CesIfo Seminar Series, Cambridge, MA, London: MIT Press, pp. 1–34.

Soskice, David (1990), 'Wage determination: the changing role of institutions in advanced industrialized countries,' *Oxford Review of Economic Policy* **6**(4), 36–61.

Steinmetz, George (2000), 'The myth of the autonomous state. Industrialists, junkers, and social policy in Imperial Germany', in Geoff Eley (ed.), *Society, Culture and the State in Germany 1870–1930*, Ann Arbor, MI: University of Michigan Press.

Steinmo, Sven (1993), *Taxation and Democracy. Swedish, British and American Approaches to Financing the Modern State*, New Haven, CT and London: Yale University Press.

Stiglitz, Joseph E. (1999), 'Taxation, public policy, and dynamics of unemployment,' *International Tax and Public Finance* **6**(3), 239–62.

Summers, Lawrence, Gruber, Jonathan and Vergara, Rodrigo (1992), 'Taxation and the structure of labor markets: the case of corporatism,' NBER Working Paper Series No. 4063.

Svallfors, S. (1997), 'Worlds of welfare and attitudes to redistribution: A comparison of eight western nations,' *European Sociological Review* **13**(3), 283–304.

Swank, Duane (2006), 'Tax policy in an era of internationalization: explaining the spread of neoliberalism,' *International Organization* **60**(4), 847–82.

Swank, Duane and Steinmo, Sven (2002), 'The new political economy of taxation in advanced capitalist democracies,' *American Journal of Political Science* **46**(3), 642–55.

Taylor, Alan J. P. (2004), *The Course of German History*, reprint of 1945 Version. London and New York: Routledge.

Tennstedt, Florian and Winter, Heidi (1993), *Von der Reichsgründungszeit bis zur kaiserlichen Sozialbotschaft (1867–1881)*, Vol. 2 of *Quellensammlung zur Geschichte der Deutschen Sozialpolitik 1867 bis 1914*, Stuttgart: Gustav Fischer.

Tilly, Charles (1966), 'The political economy of public finance and industrialization of Prussia 1815–1866,' *The Journal of Economic History* **December**, 484–97.

Titmus, Richard (1974), *Social Policy. An Introduction*, New York: Pantheon.

Towers, Brian (1989), 'Running the gauntlet: British trade unions under Thatcher, 1979–1988,' *Industrial and Labor Relations Review* **42**(2), 163–88.

Trampusch, Christine (2005), 'Institutional resettlement: the case of early retirement in Germany', in Wolfgang Streeck and Kathleen Thelen (eds), *Beyond Continuity: Institutional Change in Advanced Political Economies*, Oxford: Oxford University Press, pp. 203–28.

Traxler, Franz, Blaschke, Sabine and Kittel, Bernhard (2001), *National Labour Relations in Internationalized Markets*, Oxford: Oxford University Press.

Tsebelis, George (2002), *Veto Players. How Political Institutions Work*, New York and Princeton, NJ: Russell Sage Foundation, Princeton University Press.

Visser, Jelle (2006), 'Union membership statistics in 24 countries,' *Monthly Labour Review* **129**(1), 38–49.

Volkerink, Bjørn and de Haan, Jakob (1999), 'Political and institutional determinants of the tax mix: an empirical investigation for OECD countries,' Mimeograph January.

Volkerink, Bjørn, Sturm, Jan-Egbert and de Haan, Jakob (2002), 'Tax ratios in macroeconomics: do taxes really matter?' *Empirica* **29**, 209–24.

Wagner, Gert (1998), 'Die Reform der 620-Mark-Jobs: Stückwerk,' *DIW Wochenbericht* 49/1998.

Wagschal, Uwe (2001), 'Deutschlands Steuerstaat und die vier Welten der Besteuerung', in Manfred G. Schmidt (ed.), *Wohlfahrtsstaatliche Politik: Institutionen – Prozesse Leistungsprofil*, Opladen: Leske+Budrich, pp. 124–59.

Wagschal, Uwe (2003), 'Die politische Ökonomie der Besteuerung', in Herbert Obinger, Uwe Wagschal and Bernhard Kittel (eds), *Politische Ökonomie*, Opladen: Leske + Budrich, pp. 259–88.

Wagstaff, Adam *et al.* (1999), 'Redistributive effect, progressivity and differential tax treatment: Personal income taxes in twelve OECD countries,' *Journal of Public Economics* **72**, 73–98.

Wallich, Henry C. and Weintraub, Sidney (1971), 'A Tax-Based Incomes Policy,' *Journal of Economic Issues* **5**(2), 1–19.

Weaver, S. Roy (1914), 'Taxation in New France: a study in pioneer economics,' *Journal of Political Economy* **22**(8), 736–55.

Wehler, Hans-Ulrich (1995), *Deutsche Gesellschaftsgeschichte*, Vol. 3, München: Beck.

Wilkinson, David, Harbridge, Raymond and Walsh, Pat (2003), 'Labour market re-regulation and its effects on free-riding in New Zealand,' *Journal of Industrial Relations* **45**(4), 529–38.

Williamson, Oliver E. (1988), 'Corporate finance and corporate governance,' *Journal of Finance* **42**, 567–91.

Wilson, John Douglas (1999), 'Theories of tax competition,' *National Tax Journal* **52**(2), 269–304.

Winner, Hannes (2005), 'Has tax competition emerged in OECD countries? Evidence from panel data,' *International Tax and Public Finance* **12**(5), 667–87.

Wood, Adrian (1994), *North-South Trade, Employment and Inequality. Changing Fortunes in a Skill-Driven World*, Oxford: Clarendon.

Wooldridge, Jeffrey M. (2002), *Econometric Analysis of Cross Section and Panel Data*, Cambridge, MA: MIT Press.

Zohlnhöfer, Reimut (2001), 'Parteien, Vetospieler und der Wettbewerb um Wählerstimmen: Die Arbeitmarkt- und Beschäftigungspolitik der Ära Kohl,' *Politische Vierteljahresschrift* **42**(4), 655–82.

Zohlnhöfer, Reimut (2006), 'Vom Wirtschaftswunder zum kranken Mann Europas? Wirtschaftspolitik seit 1945', in Manfred G. Schmid and Reimut Zohlnhöfer (eds), *Regieren in der Bundesrepublik Deutschland. Innen- und Außenpolitik seit 1949*, Wiesbaden: VS Verlag für Sozialwissenschaften, pp. 285–313.

Index